The Heart of a Runaway

The Heart of a Runaway
Copyright © 1995 by Janet Chester Bly

Discovery House Publishers is affiliated with RBC Ministries,
Grand Rapids, Michigan 49512

Discovery House books are distributed to the trade by
Thomas Nelson Publishers, Nashville, Tennessee 37214

Unless otherwise indicated, Scripture is taken from the
HOLY BIBLE, NEW INTERNATIONAL VERSION.
Copyright © 1973, 1978, 1984 International Bible Society.
Used by permission of Zondervan Bible Publishers.

Library of Congress Cataloging-in-Publication Data

Bly, Janet Chester
    The heart of a runaway : hope and understanding for the woman
who longs to escape / by Janet Chester Bly.
        p.   cm.
    ISBN 0-929239-95-4
    1. Runaway wives. 2. Runaway wives—Religious life. I. Title.
    HQ759.B626   1995
    305.4—dc20   95-34024
                                                                CIP

Printed in the United States of America

95 96 97 98 99 00 / CHG / 10 9 8 7 6 5 4 3 2 1

For lists of other books, correspondence, or information about
speaking for women's groups, write:

Janet Chester Bly
P. O. Box 157
Winchester, Idaho 83555

To Louise,
for the many roads
we've gone down together.

Contents

Acknowledgments

A very special thanks and appreciation goes to the many who have helped me with this book.

- To librarian Connie Pentzer who shoved books at me as fast as she could.
- To these professionals who provided insights from their own expertise and experiences:

Judy Alexandre, Ph.D., L.C.S.W., Board Certified Diplomate

Darlene Bogle, Director, Paraklete Ministries

Cherie Collister, R.N., Personal Care Health Services

Anne Marie Ezzo, R.N., author and seminar leader on parenting issues

Beverly Mirise, Ph.D., Psychotherapist

Dr. Lynn Jones Parker, Psychotherapist, founder of Women Supporting Women

Ray W. Smith, Executive Director, The Christian Counseling Center

Linda Van Wyk, M.S.W., Therapist

- To my husband, Steve, and Jan Grueter and Darlene Bogle and Anne Marie Ezzo for their encouragement and comments and advice and willingness to read through my rough drafts.
- And last, but not least, to the women who shared so generously with me their very personal experiences.

Preface

Some of us learned it as children.

Whenever problems piled up—home got tense, we failed a test we hadn't studied for, a special boy spurned us—we threatened to run. We dreamed of the adventure, the escape route, how sorry everyone would be.

But some of us didn't do it. Where would we go? How long could we survive? What would we do after the first day? Besides, we had a change in fortune. Mom's mood improved. The test was no big deal. The football star smiled at us, acknowledged our existence for the first time. Life wasn't so bad after all.

But some of us did—pouting in our rooms, hiding at a friend's house, storming through the streets. But we got that out of our system and grew up.

Or did we?

Running can be a habit that's hard to break.

The idea to write a book on runaway women grabbed me years ago and never let me go, although at the time I didn't know any runaways personally, or so I thought, and I personally felt safe from that temptation. But as I began to speak on the subject to women's groups and talk with increasing numbers of women who wanted to run and as I entered into the private thoughts and feelings of women who had run, I recognized some common refrains in myself and realized that we're all potential runaways!

Life is tough, even when we're basically content. Life is complex, even if we don't consider the added mix of the strife of emotions that stir inside us. Life is short, and we want to do so much. And each of us has her fragile edge, her cramped corners, her longing to be free. Life is harsh and some will run. And the ones left behind bear the brunt of guilt, workload, and rejection.

One bit of warning: this book is meant for those who are ready to read it. It's voluntary, personal choice material for people who say, "I am here!" or "I know someone who's there; how can I help?" If this book is handed to you by someone who says, "You really need this," read several lines and (a) continue reading, (b) return to sender, (c) pass it on to someone who's trying hard to read the title as you walk past, or who puts it back quickly when you enter the room, or who has that stricken, *How did you know?* look when you give a book review at a retreat or board meeting.

One bit of advice: the reader will gain the most benefit from this book by answering and discussing the questions at the end of the chapters with a friend or support group. The questions are an important part of the material. This is not a "how to" book. It's a resource for provoking thought and action. The questions help the reader complete in her own mind what the subject of running away and the plight of those who flee has to do with her.

Janet Chester Bly
Winchester, Idaho

One

No Time to Pack Photo Albums or Heirlooms

You may be a runaway. And know it. Or refuse to admit it.

You may know a runaway. One who is driving you crazy.

Runaways come from high-rises and flatlands, from holes in the wall and ranch houses, from tenements and estates. A runaway may be the owner of a corporation or a homeless person shuffling down a midnight city street. That one may be known as a father, or brother, or son; a sister, or daughter, or wife.

He could be your mailman. She could be your coworker.

Or she could be you.

We almost expect the young to run—teens needing space, freedom to find themselves. They're working through hormone attacks. Or finding their separate identity. They're the moody adolescents, the rebels, the problem children. They can be anti-authority, or truly abused. They can be malcontents, or suffocated with doting love. They can be neglected, or overdisciplined. But they think the only solution is to get out of where they are.

Men have joined the ranks of runaways—those who abandon homes for secretaries or midlife flings. Those who abscond with company funds. Those who renounce political loyalties and defect from their country—the deserters of war duty. A growing number are delinquent in alimony payments and child care obligations.

Kids and dads and husbands and men under terrific pressure sometimes feel the need to run.

But women are catching up. There's a whole new class of runaways.

> It is true, more men than women still do desert families. But numerically the male-female runaway gap is swiftly closing. During the past decade and a half more married women were reported "missing" than in the entire previous existence of the L.A.P.D.'s Missing Persons Bureau, and this alarming statistic is surprisingly consistent throughout the nation.[1]

On a dreary, drizzly, foggy day in January, 1979, Elaine Nelson Thompson ran away from home. She left behind a husband of eighteen years and four children: Toni, 5, Jenni, 7, Charles Stanley, 10, and Anna Mae, 17.

She had plenty of reasons, but was too beaten down at the time to explain them.

Her church family soundly condemned her. Her husband demanded that she come back. Her siblings and parents disowned her. Meanwhile she struggled with chronic illness and deep depression while holding onto a weak will to live in what seemed to be a harsh and loveless world.

The sin of desertion was the transgression that convinced all her accusers that she was totally to blame. They could make clear exactly what she'd done wrong, but no one could show her—because of the depths of her pain and despair—how to make things right.

She couldn't get well. Her commitments had overextended her resources and energies. She felt oppression at home and misunderstood in the church and community. Those few who made the effort to face her expressed condemnation. Their ungracious attitudes fed her view that everyone around her was critical, that no one cared. No one understood her desperate need for healing, hope, and wholeness. So she remained a runaway.[2]

But running away doesn't always mean leaving home. Some hide there instead. Some live in a dream world of delusion and self-deception. Others find a fast track that attempts to obliterate sights and sounds and revelations they're trying to avoid. They're not fully alert to the stark now, the pregnant present. They're emotionally and mentally on the run.

Some are just trying to find home.

Where is "home" really?

If home is finally found, do some keep right on running, because that's always been their habit? Or is home just too difficult to recognize, the first time around?

Dr. Judy Alexandre describes a runaway as "an adult with responsibilities, such as marriage, children, job, who chooses to leave with no mutual agreement, plan, or goal."[3]

Counselor Darlene Bogle puts it another way: "An adult runaway is any adult who abdicates the position of responsibility in the social/family structure that is traditionally ascribed to that individual."[4]

An adult runaway, for the purposes of this book's discussion, is defined as anyone who abruptly and willfully withdraws emotional and/or physical support from a commitment, covenant, or responsibility, without adequate cooperation, explanation, or consideration for those left behind.

There are three main categories of adult runaways:

1. *Potential.* One engrossed in runaway thinking patterns.

2. *Actual.* One who has exhibited runaway behavior either as a one-time event or as a chronic response to life.
3. *Reformed.* One who has been potential or actual, but is now becoming a stander.

A *stander* is a woman who consciously or unconsciously has a habit of saying, "I am here! This *X* marks my spot. To the best of my ability I will erect a positive construction from the materials handed me or from those I have chosen."

A *wanderer* is one type of chronic runner. She hasn't found her home yet, or doesn't want one, or perhaps she found her place once, lost it, and is searching for it again. Her mind's easily interrupted, distracted, detoured.

A *stay-at-home runaway* copes by pulling inside, by creating a dream world that she deems perfect for her, one that safely contradicts her real world. She runs from an honest encounter with her needs and frank discussions of opportunities that might promote growth in her present relationships. There's the constant drudge of duty, the monotony of the menial. Ruts and routines could give way to stimulation and freshness. There's a longing for freedom, for a way of escape.

Eloise is that kind of runaway. From her upstairs bedroom window she spends hours watching the neighbors, studying their activities and visitors and cracking open the window to catch snatches of conversations. She's depressed or joyful, depending on what's happening to her soap-opera characters. She nags her husband for bits of gossip from the plant where he works. She can't stand to be alone without some kind of noise blaring—the radio, the TV, the dishwasher—anything. She reads *National Inquirer* and *Soap Opera Digest* religiously to learn of the problems of strangers. However, when her sister calls to tell her she's going to have cancer surgery, Eloise crawls in bed for three days.

A *throwaway* is another kind of runaway. She is the one who, rather than run *herself*, rids herself of the offending party. Her victims include the young, the elderly, and other discardables.

Kim was only sixteen. She didn't do drugs. But she did have a dealer. She was an addicted gambler, and her mother couldn't bear the lying and stealing and cheating anymore. Sports betting, card playing, lotteries—Kim squandered every cent on her compulsion. her mother booted her out. Now Kim is considered the runaway.

To run away is a decisive pulling out (often shocking, sudden to onlookers), leaving behind an unresolved conflict or incomplete closure or unfulfilled obligation. Those who are affected see it as abandonment, a betrayal of trust or loyalty.

The runaway, however, may not see her action in the same light. She may have been thinking through the leaving process for a long time and be quite used to the idea, "acting out the running that has gone on inside her for years."[5] She can be quite amazed that everyone hasn't guessed what she had in mind, especially when it's possible she thought that her only other alternatives were submission to a beaten down existence or suicide.

It's very hard to consider oneself a runaway unless (a) one is forced to face the brunt of some of the consequences of running, or (b) one embraces a higher motive, insight, or purpose that helps define the action by a different standard.

Yet, the Bible says we're all runaways.

> We all, like sheep, have gone astray,
> each of us has turned to his own way.
>
> Isaiah 53:6

We're all in this together. We're like a bunch of dumb sheep. We get lost. We wander—sometimes far from home. Each of us has her own way of straying. We just have a very difficult time recognizing our personal wayward paths. We're too busy looking outward, paying attention to the wanderings of others. But left completely on our own, with no thought of a higher standard or the welfare of others, would we run, too?

We All Like Sheep

Why do we run away? And why do we find it so difficult to discern runaway behavior in ourselves?

We all have times when we need to stand aside, take a look at ourselves, "to recall myself, recover, return."[6]

Is it because we're angry? Is it because we're under the control of dark moods? Is it because it's an alternative to suicide?

Is it because we become undermined, or overloaded?

Is it because we've come under a dominant negative influence?

Is it because we're repeating a generational pattern?

Is it because we define commitment as "taking care of me"? Is it because we see all relationships and situations as "temporary"?

Is it because we're trapped by an addiction?

Is it because we're trying to undo foolish choices? We want a chance to start over again?

Is it because we're hiding from something?

Is it because we're weighed down with debts? Overloaded with commitments? Cut down by criticism? Burned out on burdens?

Is it because life's so unfair? Or we've been terribly wounded?

Is it because of an intolerable circumstance, or abusive person? Do we desperately need release from some stress?

Is it because we're looking for attention?

Is it because we need a change in who we are, in who we're known as?

Is it because the enticements "out there" outweigh the rewards of faithfulness "where I'm at"?

Is it because we're swayed by passions and desire—sin?

Is it because we're lonely? Depressed? Or just plain bored?

Is it because of guilt or shame?

Is it because of unresolved conflicts?

Is it because of a feeling of failure, that we've accomplished nothing, that we're going nowhere?

Is it because we want revenge, we need to retaliate?

Is it because that's the only thing we have the courage to do?

Is it because it is our conviction that this is our only means of survival?

Maybe we want an easy way out.

Or is it because of love?

A woman who runs must fight basic fears: fear of loss, fear of the unknown, fear of leaving the familiar, fear of failure. She's got to be desperate to leave. She's got to feel out of control—whether undone by raging emotions, or intolerable living conditions, or physical imbalances, or neglect of some vital disciplines.

We won't know for sure until we study the heart of a runaway.

But just as important, we need to know the heart of a heavenly Father who loves and reasons and maneuvers His runaway children home.

Discovery Questions

1. Describe an adult runaway in your own words.

2. Has someone close to you ever run away?
   If so, what was/is your response?

3. Have you ever thought about running away?
   If so, why?
   Where would you go? What would you do?

4. Why do you think there are more women runaways today than ever before?

5. What would you say to someone who was contemplating a run?

6. What would you say to someone who has already run?

7. Read Psalm 139:7–12.
   What are the assurances? What are the warnings?

Notes

[1]Don Rowell, "Adult Runaways," *America*, 30 January 1982, 70.
[2]Elaine Nelson Thompson, interview by author.
[3]Judy Alexandre, in correspondence with author, January, 1992.
[4]Darlene Bogle, in correspondence with author, January 1992.
[5]Ibid.
[6]Esther de Waal, *A Seven Day Journey with Thomas Merton* (Ann Arbor, Mich.: Servant, 1992), 58.

Two

See Why We Run

I rarely meet a woman who hasn't wanted to run. Sometime. From something. For some reason.

Some never will, but they want their feelings understood by a significant individual. They long for another human to enter into their world for a time and see what it looks like from their view—the sights and sounds and sensations.

But some have run and need a way back, to a place they can call home. A place of pardon. A place of restitution. A place in the church. A place of peace with themselves and God. A place for confession, repentance, forgiveness, and love.

One day Elaine, in a dazed stupor, found herself staring at a freeway billboard advertising a mental health clinic. She drove to the address, was put on tranquilizers, and then placed into a group where participants droned on about the gory details of their existence. "This wasn't what I wanted. I recognized for the first time my desperate need for help, but had nowhere to turn.

"I was very sick—later I learned I had pneumonia. My marriage had been a sham for years. My church was going through a terrible upheaval. So many looked to me for strength. I was the cheery one, the one who got things done, the ready helper. They couldn't see me dying inside and I didn't know how to tell them."

23

One night her husband returned from work to find her gone. Elaine could think of no other solution to her misery except to vanish, to leave it all behind, to stop trying anymore.

"I couldn't take the kids. I wasn't emotionally, mentally, or physically equipped. Besides, he made a generous income; the home was his. What kind of life would they have with me?"

All the time Elaine was running she sought God. She cried out to Him. "I always felt the presence of the Lord and experienced His protection," she recalls, "but confusion reigned. I didn't know where I fit, where I belonged, or what to plan on. I just didn't know where 'home' was for me anymore."

I just didn't know where home was.

How can we know where *home* truly is for any of us?

There's a saying that home is where your stuff is.

Another suggests that it's where charity begins.

T. S. Eliot says it's where one starts from.

O. Henry says it's not appreciated until you've left it.

And Thomas Wolfe intimated that once you leave it, you can't really ever go back.

Many who run seek home through one of three driving passions:

- fulfilling relationships
- pursuit of dreams or ambitions
- personal peace

Relationships

Isolation can happen to full-time homemakers or career women. Commitment to professional success doesn't leave much time for socializing outside the workplace. It's common and expected at successful companies, such as in the Silicon Valley, to work fourteen to sixteen hours a day, seven days a week. These kinds of jobs often lure workers who have no extended family in the area. When stress and exhaustion hits, they're alone.[1]

Our society as a whole has moved away from the family network of reunions and get-togethers that once held clans together. Today, many families don't even know aunts, uncles, or cousins. And rarely are they close to the ones they do know. We make our way through life largely alone.

We attempt to gain our identity from contacts with our significant others. Everyone has multiple identities: student, worker, friend, parent, daughter, spouse. And these identities can conflict on a daily basis. Even marriage partners can be sleeping with strangers if they're mismatched in their ideas about themselves and each other.

When a woman has a feeling of a minimal existence—of being lost in the dark, of wanting more than she's got, of feeling that she's invisible, with no impact on anyone, watching the world from a distance, concluding that she's a has been, her glory days gone, and one other human being makes her feel special, alive—she's gone!

"There's a big difference between being busy and being connected," says Evelyn Moschetta, D.S.W., a New York-based psychotherapist. "Many women today are very, very busy, but they don't have enough truly genuine relationships, people with whom they can be totally open, who accept and love them for who they really are. That's the basis of real friendship. And it's missing today in a fundamental way."[2]

"In our society, loneliness is a secret we keep—sometimes even from ourselves," says Anne Peplau, Ph.D., a professor of social psychology at UCLA who has studied the subject for twenty years. "Loneliness has a stigma attached to it. There's an assumption out there that if you're lonely, it must be your own fault.

Otherwise, you'd certainly have lots of friends, right?"[3]

At a recent women's conference, in a prayer group of eleven, a well-dressed, attractive elderly woman admitted, "I just lost my husband several months ago and at my age I know that's to be expected. But I'm not ashamed to admit that I'm lonely."

Her frankness encouraged the other women not only to reach out to her, but to open up about their own problems and needs. A meeting that had been scheduled for forty-five minutes stretched into several hours.

What are some of the aspects that entice us into relationships?

- freedom
- the need to "do something for myself"
- adventure
- a sense of redeeming wasted time
- variety
- romance
- a haven in a hostile, brutal world
- affirmation
- a listening heart to expound, ponder, complain to
- absence of conflict
- pleasure
- stimulation

A new friend can restore for us what we once had or add something we have never experienced. Old relationships can burn out by faults that are never corrected, strains that are never smoothed out, and all the other rigorous disciplines of the long haul that lifetime commitments require.

Alice had been married over twenty years. She felt unfulfilled by her husband and got involved physically with a woman friend. Plagued by guilt, she ended the affair, but in her mind she kept the fantasies alive. She functioned sexually for her husband, but only because she imagined she was with her female lover. She was still home, but she had run sexually, morally, and spiritually, for the oneness in the marriage bond had been broken.[4]

Most who run don't leave alone. Companions can provide an added incentive and even possible resources for fleeing.

We crave love—"to love and be loved, to nurture and be nurtured, to bond . . . to be in relationships that are good, that are healthy, that are growing, that are durable"[5]—we all relate to that.

"I never saw my Dad after I was twelve years old," Dena told me. "Mom was always working or tired or with a boyfriend. My kid brothers scrambled to make it on the streets. I'm never going back there. I don't want any of that for my life. But I'm not sure what I do want. I know I don't want to wake up some day, thirty-five years old, with no family."

Dena can't find home behind her or ahead of her. Meanwhile, she's on the run—on a search, on a quest. "Women's psychological equilibrium depends on human connection. The terror for women is isolation."[6]

Dreams and Ambitions

If the meaning of life has become doubtful, if one's relations to others and to oneself do not offer security, then fame is one means to silence one's doubts.[7]

Many who run are "restive individuals," reacting to "a desperate urge to change their lives in some way."[8]

The need to try one's luck, to swim or sink, to try out the competition, to be confronted with the choice of overcoming or being overcome; success to some means economic independence. The world seems limitless.

A new environment, different people, a revised identity, a fresh start that "enables them to become finally the persons their previous existence prevented them from being."[9]

Ashley Judd, daughter of country singer Naomi Judd, revealed in an interview, "We were always covering new ground, because Mom was running away from something and looking for something at the same time."[10]

Peggy was widowed suddenly when her husband was killed in a logging accident. She and her family had lived in the small Northwest community for only a year and had made few friends. However, the town's people rallied around her and the three children with provisions and offers of service.

A few months later they were astounded when she disappeared, leaving the children behind with her elderly father-in-law. She left no forwarding address, no note, no trace. Her rented house was completely cleaned out, the children's belongings stashed in the garage where the landlord found them.

One day the husband's great aunt came to check on the kids (now in a foster home). She mentioned to an inquiring neighbor, "Those were her stepkids, you know. I think she always felt awkward with them, having no children of her own. Without Donald, I assume she felt overwhelmed."

The discovery that the kids weren't her own flesh and blood lessened the condemnation somewhat. Peggy was fleeing an existence for which she felt inadequate, to follow a dream that finally seemed possible to realize. But at a cost. Running always has a price tag.

When we fervently want something and that desire seems to be thwarted by people or circumstances or standards we can't seem to live up to, we're tempted to run.

The family is the one institution in our society that is most likely to assign roles and responsibilities solely on the basis of age and gender, instead of interest and competence. A woman can feel trapped by past commitments, by social and emotional obligations, and by her lack of alternatives.[11] She can suffer from feeling trapped like "a cog in a large machine, an automaton, that (her) life has become empty and lost its meaning."[12]

"I think more than anything it is the feeling of insignificance," says counselor Darlene Bogle, "and wanting that sense of worth through personal achievement that they feel is hindered by commitment to another."

The women's movements have tried to put a woman's frustration into sharp focus. "Those frustrations were already there," says author Myron Brenton. "As women gain more education, more awareness, more sophisticated job skills and a greater potential for careers, they come to expect more satisfactions for themselves."[13]

At the same time, these new freedoms bring a strange kind of imprisonment—the pressure's on to be competent in everything: at home, at work, involvement in the community. Many women feel snubbed by a kind of "class-consciousness . . . professional women only need apply."[14]

Just like men, women can become obsessed with education, with upward mobility, with the comforts of middle- or upper-class lifestyles. Women can feel the pressure to pursue a kind of Priscilla Principle that rivals the Peter Principle. They strive for higher and higher status jobs just because they feel they have something to prove, not because the work itself seems desirable or satisfying nor because it provides room for all the other needs in her life.

My friend Cherie explains: "It's not enough to be 'as good as' men; we have to be better. Winning these battles requires huge investments of time and energy . . .

and money. Live-in nannies are required for long over-time hours and frequent business trips."

Women must publicly demonstrate their courage, display their authority, chart their own courses, whether or not it's good for them personally. To show any kind of weakness, emotionally or professionally, means not only personal failure, but the failure of an entire gender.

The stresses are just as strong for the stay-at-homes. If you don't have a career, you must be *really good* doing the homemaking arts: sewing, cleaning, basket-weaving, canning, interior decorating, potty training, plumbing, coupon saving, silver polishing, birthday party creating, gourmet cooking. Otherwise, you'd have a *real* job.

"I never could measure up," Cynthia sighed. "My husband wanted a body like Cheryl Tiegs and a cook like Julia Childs. I've looked more like Julia since our third baby, but without her skills. I couldn't take the con-stant nags and suffering through the roller-coaster diets that never worked. I didn't like myself anymore, and neither did he. So, I dropped out. I drank until nothing bothered me anymore."

For a long time Cynthia resigned herself to hope-lessness, an either/or mindset: "Either I'm everything he wants, or I'm nothing."

However, Cynthia found a better way out. She grad-ually entered into the fellowship of a Bible study support group that included women who were spiritual encour-agers and practical helpers. She grew in knowledge of who she was in God's eyes and learned to manage her home in a way that fit her abilities and temperament.

"Two of the women even came to my house and gave it a good scrubbing so I could catch up again. They offered me their easy, tasty recipes that my whole family enjoys. I'm still tied to the house, but I'm learning tricks to make it . . . almost fun."

A woman wants to run when she's overloaded, undersupported, superstressed. Lois Braverman suggests that "the painful reality [is] that in the majority of two job marriages with young children, women [are] working a second shift—a month of 24 hour days . . . . These women [talk] about sleep the way a hungry person talks about food."[15]

For whatever reason a woman works, she usually wants shared responsibility of housework tasks and emotional and physical support in the care of children, or the desperation can become overwhelming. She may seek her fortunes elsewhere, where there are no meal deadlines, no umpteen cries of "Mama" in the night, no love demands.

Personal Peace

A young woman made her peace with God and immediately began a ministry to homeless families by inviting them into her own home. It was too much, too soon. With the inevitable stress of the confusion and commotion, she was enticed by her former drug buddies into her old lifestyle.

She ran on Mother's Day.

Her husband found her six weeks later and urged her back. Her ministry to homeless families ended while she rebuilt her own life.

She desperately sought release from worry, from tension, from decision making, from mounds of laundry and dishes—from being needed too much by too many people.

Utterly forgotten. Left without a trace. Lost to the world. Just to hide in an obscure, forgotten hole somewhere, unaware of anything or anyone—that's the desire of someone who feels she's not just "in a rut, but a chasm."[16]

A runaway hopes to improve her lot, not worsen it.

She sees her present situation as undesirable, intolerable, unlivable. She longs to be swallowed up, by any means, in quiet, blissful numbness.

A few years ago a friend who is a pastor's wife and I were laughing at a cartoon we found in *Leadership* magazine. A frazzled pastor's wife is reading the dictionary to her husband. "Well, I'll be!" she says. "They're right; here it is: 'perfect: adj. complete in all respects; without defect or omission; flawless; like a pastor, his wife, and their children.' "[17]

We hooted and howled. Then, my friend stopped and flopped down on a couch. "That is too painfully true," she confessed. "How I would love to get out of my glass house and be an anonymous citizen, just enjoy the pure exhilaration of being a normal person who nobody knows and nobody *watches*."

Some potential runaways have the feeling of constant invasion.

The Breaking Point

Inability to cope comes at different times, under different circumstances for each individual. It can be one major event. Or a pile of smaller episodes. The spirit becomes crushed. The will is weakened. Running seems the only bearable thing to do.

"I couldn't face one more morning of going through the motions. I felt everyone just take and take and take; I didn't get anything in return. All I could see, think, or feel was the moment I died inside. If only he hadn't . . . if only she could . . . if only I was . . . if only I had . . . if only . . . ."

Peace is needed, until the shock slackens, the turmoil ebbs, the horror eases. One woman explained, "It's like declaring bankruptcy. I could start with a clean slate." But sooner or later the runaway must face the past if she is to make any progress in the present.

Elaine Nelson Thompson knew she needed outside help, but any kind of counseling was fearful for her, "Until I had friends who would come alongside, would go through the process with me. It was going to open up a terrible wound that would leave me very vulnerable to hurt. I wanted to come out on the other side so strong that nothing could ever shake my relationships and commitments again."

Elaine recognized that, potentially, her running days weren't over. "Even today, when I sense rejection and misunderstanding, I want out of there. I want to be gone. My past, even in my childhood, has always been devastating. And I know it's all connected somehow. Sometimes I suffer terrible flashbacks of the fear I felt as a young girl and, later, adult scenes of cruelty. I began to believe no one could go through this with me."

Elaine is discovering that deliverance is a process. Step-by-step she's doing the next thing God shows her to do. And each step brings another piece of the place she can embrace as her home.

"I still have my trials. But like my theme verses in 2 Corinthians 1:3–4, I'm looking for opportunities to comfort others in trouble as I myself have been comforted. The most urgent need I had during my long siege of mental and emotional darkness was for fellow believers who would reach out to me, to love me and understand me when they perceived that I was doing something wrong."[18]

God loves the runaway.

He comes to meet us where we are.

He sought out Adam and Eve hiding in the bushes. He comforted Hagar in the desert when she ran from her abusive mistress. He found and conversed with Elijah huddled in a cave for fear of Jezebel. He reasoned with the pouting Jonah on the hilltop while he still fought the

Lord's will. He raised up an imprisoned Paul to speak for Onesimus, the runaway slave.

And He's using friends, prayer partners, and a loving church family to extend His mercy to Elaine.

She's no longer a runaway.

Discovery Questions

1. When under extreme stress, how do you cope?
   Has this been a good method for you? Why?
   What would be a better action to practice?

2. Which woman illustrated in these first two chapters do you most relate to, and why?

3. Are there biblical age and gender roles?
   Explain, with scriptural references.

4. Read Psalm 55.
   Have you ever endured anything like this?
   What lesson did you learn that you could share to encourage others?

Notes

[1]Cherie Collister, in correspondence with author, March 1992.

[2]Ibid.

[3]Margery D. Rosen, "All Alone: The New Loneliness of American Women," *Ladies Home Journal,* April 1991, 216.

[4]Bogle, letter.

[5]Myron Brenton, *Lasting Relationships: How to Recognize the Man or Woman Who's Right for You* (New York: A & W Publishers, 1981), 2–3.

[6]Anastasia Toufexis, "Coming from a Different Place," *Time,* 1990, 64.

[7]Erich Fromm, *Escape from Freedom* (New York: Holt, Rinehart and Winston, 1941), 49.

[8]Rowell, "Adult Runaways," 69.

[9]Ibid.

[10]Ashley Judd, "The Day I Finally Told Mom about My Dream," interview by Gail Buchalter, *Parade,* 22 August 1993, 4.

[11]Walter R. Gove, Carolyn Briggs Style, and Michael Hughes, "The Effect of Marriage on the Well-Being of Adults," *Journal of Family Issues* 11, no. 1 (March 1990): 22–23.

[12]Fromm, *Escape from Freedom,* 276.

[13]Brenton, *The Runaways: Children, Husbands, Wives, and Parents* (Boston: Little, Brown, 1978), 124.

[14]Dorcas J. Bethel, in "Letters," *Moody,* April 1992, 10.

[15]Lois Braverman, "The Dilemma of Housework," *Journal of Marital and Family Therapy* (January 1991): 26.

[16]Elizabeth Cody Newenhuyse, *Sometimes I Feel Like Running Away from Home* (Minneapolis: Bethany House, 1992), 143.

[17]Steve Phelps, cartoon, *Leadership* (Spring 1988): 3.

[18]E. N. Thompson, interview.

Three

Celeste Doesn't Love Here Anymore
How to Recognize a Potential Runaway

Celeste drove a mail truck, served as flower chairman for her church, and seemed dedicated to her husband and five sons. She claimed several women as fairly close friends, and though she could be moody at times, she appeared to have few problems.

Then Pierce, her four-year-old, drowned in the family pool. Six months later her husband, Ben, was fired from a job he'd held for fourteen years.

Celeste's friends and church rallied around the family. Words of sympathy. Gifts of food. Even loan offers. But Celeste rebuffed attempts to talk about Pierce or their financial hardships. Some thought she was brave and strong. Others sensed she wanted to be left alone, so she could think things through.

Celeste got out of the house less and less. Ben was seen pushing the grocery cart and taking the boys to Sunday school. Her friends tried calling or stopping by, but her lack of warm response discouraged them. Her unkempt house surprised and concerned them. However, if they offered help, she responded with hostility; if they left her alone, she complained that they didn't care.

Then Brenda, an acquaintance from high school days, became a constant presence. With no children, a nice income from alimony settlements and real estate deals, Brenda had a lot of time, and she began to spend it with Celeste.

One day after an argument (about the attention Brenda got compared to the family), Ben returned home to find Celeste gone and a note on the table: "You can reach me at Brenda's. I'm not coming back. Please don't try."

Her family and friends were dumbfounded. They had no clue, no warning.

Or did they?

Is it possible to recognize signals that a woman is contemplating a run?

Of course, no one profile fits all cases. If we want to hide our intentions, we probably can. But these general symptoms will stir insights into a growing number of runaways.

Problems Coping with Central Life Issues

"Then Pierce, her four-year-old, drowned in the family pool. Six months later her husband, Ben, was fired from a job he'd held for fourteen years."

A potential runaway wants to vanish from public view. She may feel like a victim, completely controlled by outside conditions. Her stress levels are low and her coping mechanisms are stunted because of the severity of her circumstances or the weakened condition of her mind, body, or spirit.

It may begin with fear—that life's out of her control, that nothing can be counted on, that anything you really care about can be lost. This leads to frustration, then a fantasy world, an ideal dream existence where nothing can touch her or leave her, where she's in control and can grab what she wants when she wants it.

A crucial relationship has soured. Thoughtless remarks dig deep. She feels unwanted or unneeded. A potential runaway wrestles with the quality of her relationships. Friends don't seem to understand or truly want to help. They're busy, detached, wanting her to quickly snap out of it. She doesn't understand herself either. She's in a daze, doesn't care about things anymore. She's easily angered. Prone to panic. She begins to store up resentments. She's easily influenced by anyone who will stick with her, show her steady and nonjudgmental attention, show her a way out of her confusion.

A potential runaway may be frustrated with her ability to pursue ambitions. Goals or dreams appear out of reach. She has no clear sense of purpose or direction and senses little cooperation or support from significant others.

She's in the spotlight of a crunching dilemma that demoralizes her; she doesn't know how to handle it. She's unable to think things through, to find an orderly pattern to what's happening. Her roller-coaster existence has worn her out; she's just plain exhausted.

A caring observer would also be open to signs of violence or abuse.

Gradual Emotional Withdrawal

"Celeste rebuffed attempts to talk about Pierce or their financial hardships. . . . [She] got out of the house less and less."

The potential runaway gradually reduces emotional and physical involvement in key relationships. Less affection. Less attention and warmth. Less contact. Alienation. The evidence is in the contrast. She was once a contented, happy woman most of the time. Now, she's sullen or drops out of things she cared about before. She had a life, now she's pulling back.

As she pulls away, she perceives herself as being left out. She feels neglected. She's prone to alternating periods of depression and elation. She loses interest in activities and people she formerly enjoyed or valued. At times she looks lost, restless, or confused.

Privately she indulges in runaway fantasies—where she would run, how she would do it, the feelings of freedom, forging a new identity, the peace, the hope, something lost recaptured.

> In general, becoming a runaway is conceived as a process of action and reaction, which unfolds over time. Becoming a runaway is the end product of a person's actions, reason, and symbols.[1]

Running away often begins long before the actual event. A lot of preparation takes place in first softening, then hardening and setting the emotions and will into the heart of a runaway.

Alert observers will see the signs.

There's a change in behavior or outlook. Excuses may be common. Prolonged contact with family and friends is avoided. Complaints about flaws and faults increase. Busyness escalates with the emotional withdrawal.

> Not that everyone who leads a seemingly busy life is a potential runaway. But when people make new or newly vigorous efforts to absent themselves from their families, it frequently does tend to be a sign that something is seriously wrong.[2]

The runaway can be a loner, a stranger to those around her. Aloof, inward, she hides her feelings and opinions. A brooder, one who gives cautious smiles, she may see herself as a victim of misfortunes.

On the other hand, she can be pleasant, but rarely reveals her true concerns or problems. She may be quick to deny she has any problems at all. Her anger may be passive and inward.

One counselor sees the runaway as "one who is desperate . . . low self-esteem, usually very little college or job experience, someone who has very few friends, who is dependent, fearful, and desperate."[3]

An outsider can judge the depressed as lazy, sad, and blue. The tendency is to tell her to snap out of it. But there could be deep problems from the past that hold her in bondage. Or she could have a chemical imbalance that requires medical attention. Or both. Some problems need professional expertise. Others benefit from a change in routine.

Someone Else's Life Looks Better

"Then Brenda, an acquaintance from high school days, became a constant presence. With no children, a nice income from alimony settlements and real estate deals, Brenda had a lot of time, and she began to spend it with Celeste."

The runaway sometimes needs a partner, someone who can feed the direction her mind has begun to take, someone who can give her extra impetus. Former friends are shut out. Or shut her out. She draws to herself those with a similar mindset. This partner may provoke increasing conflict in the present problem, as well as offer her a route out of it. It may even come down to an either/or confrontation.

Much like other forms of social behavior, becoming a runaway demands exposure to the actions and attitudes of others en route to learning the runaway role.

Exposure helps shape this role, allows individuals to identify with the role.[4]

Role models are important to a runaway. They provide a stimulus for such concrete actions as stashing money, investigating job openings in distant towns, scouting alternative living quarters, and testing her runaway partner's intentions. Serious plans are made without panic, with a growing sense of peace that she's finally in charge of her life. She tries to cover all the contingencies and all the deliberation and plotting settles her mind and resolve. A sense of excitement replaces former days of gloom and despair. A partner adds strength—of resources and will—and promises relief from an unbearable aloneness.

She's much more sensitive to criticism. She finds it hard to see anything positive about her present situation. She may have no clear direction for the future, but knows she's unhappy with the present. She's at the stage of "exploring, testing, and defining [her] limits."[5]

Running may bring freedom, may bring fun, may provide a new love interest. It's a mental health adventure. But it has long-term consequences.

Conflicts Take on Dramatic Implications

"One day after an argument [about the attention Brenda got, compared to the family], Ben returned home to find Celeste gone."

Any problems may seem to justify her position that the present situation is impossible. Adversity will sharpen her desire to run and provide a further defense on her behalf: tight finances, a sudden loss, an unwelcome change, headaches, a snub, a milestone birthday, negative news.

Unwillingness to Aggressively Seek Other Solutions

"However, if they offered help, she responded with hostility; if they left her alone, she complained that they didn't care."

She has talked herself into most every stage except the actual running. She's in no mood to accept advice or counsel that would suggest another option. She builds herself into a world of "shrinking alternatives."[6] With this boxed-in thinking, interest in discussing her situation or inner struggles decreases, except as a means of defense for her chosen plan of escape. Fleeing is seen as the only way to protect or vindicate herself, though no part of her main problem—besides cessation of immediate conflict—will be solved. Pessimism toward everyone and everything, other than the possible runaway partner and runaway procedure, dominates.

She may run to escape unbearable pressure. She's locked into thinking patterns which tell her that her problem-solving options are limited, and none of these will work. There is no way out. She feels the primary burden for managing these problems is upon her, and she wants relief from the burden. She feels her best efforts will never be enough to resolve key issues (and she may be right). With this failure projection tightly woven, she desires to creep away quietly, do some small thing that promises a measure of success.[7]

The Practice Runs

Frequently runaways start to run for some time before actually disappearing. Theirs are trial runs, so to speak.[8]

She comes home later than usual. She increases involvement with meetings, clubs, or a friend. She may make trips home to Mom or take long lunch hours. There's an unexplained overnighter, or headaches that keep her in bed all day. She spends hours in front of the TV, or weeks in romantic novels.

The potential runaway may talk about it first, another form of practicing, a kind of warning. The response she receives will either encourage or discourage her further plans.

There's an effort to tidy up details. "For example," home nurse Cherie Collister has observed, "the mother may make sure that the childcare situation is good, or that medical records are complete, so that adequate care will continue. This is similar to a person contemplating suicide—taking care of unfinished business.[9]

Maryanne discovered her runaway tendencies in a much different way.

One stormy night she raced home through the country roads to catch her traveling husband's weekly telephone call. Suddenly, in the headlights, there appeared a boy on a bike. She swerved, too late, and felt the crunch. In a moment of panic, she kept going. She was on the run. All the stages of running away rolled into one massive grip of fear—fear of facing what was behind her, fear of blame, fear of being caught, fear of public ridicule. The longer she hesitated, the harder it was to turn back. And the car rushed on.

A woman runs and we're shocked.

Then the dust settles and we wonder, *What was she thinking? What was in her heart that she'd do such a thing?*

Her motives are mysteries. Her pain is hidden. We're not privy to that inside information: the irritations, the frustrations, the abuses behind closed doors. We're the company in front of whom she used a different voice.

Does she have regrets? How will she make things right? How should I respond to her? Will understanding make it easier to forgive? But what about all the others who were hurt? Will understanding help me recognize the runaway heart inside myself? All we have left to assess is the facade, the shadow image, and the signs— the signs we could have discerned much sooner, to reach out in some way, if we'd only known.

Discovery Questions

1. If you had been Celeste's friend, what would you have done and why?

2. What do you think is the very best thing a caring observer could do for a woman who is planning to run?

3. Who were you most concerned for, and why? Celeste? Ben? The boys? Brenda? The friends? The church members? Who most upset you?

4. What runaway behavior/stage do you recognize in yourself?

5. What type of situation would most provoke you to want to run? Who would you take with you? What would be your end goal?

Notes

[1] Joseph E. Palenski and Harold M. Launer, "The 'Process' of Running Away: A Redefinition," *Adolescence* 22, no. 86 (Summer 1987): 347.

[2] Brenton, *The Runaways,* 16.

[3] Lynn Jones Parker, in correspondence with the author, January 1992.

[4] Palenski and Launer, "Running Away," 348.

[5] Ibid., 349.

[6] Ibid., 354.

[7] Collister, letter.

[8] Brenton, *The Runaways,* 15.

[9] Collister, letter.

Four

Shelter in a Time of Storm
Befriending a Runaway: Part One

Maxine whisked her five children out of the house and hid them in the homes of various friends and relatives who would later make permanent arrangements for each child. She wouldn't allow her accomplices to tell her the final destinations for the children, so her husband couldn't beat it out of her.

She stayed at home until each was safely hidden away, while trying to keep her husband distracted, unaware, and calm. Then she fled.

Maxine refused to stay with anyone her husband knew, in order to protect the kids and hide herself. She applied for public assistance and waited several months before trying to contact the children. "If he found me, I wanted them unreachable."

She had grown so accustomed to and fearful of her husband's violent rages and threats that she waited a full year before she gathered her children together.

How easily we cheer Maxine and her difficult task of safety and protection for her loved ones. But the backdrop for runaways is much wider in scope, with a more encompassing range of circumstances and impulses and incentives. And in other cases our mercy may bleed very thin indeed.

What's a Woman Expected To Be?

When we think of a woman facing obstacles, challenges, conflicts, what do we assume she'll do? Especially if children are involved?

Isn't part of the glory of being female the ability to display the virtues of nurturer and peacemaker, to stand by her man, to fight like a lioness for her young, or to become a sacrificial lamb? Or are these images meant to keep us in our place? Even when that place doesn't fit? Or are they biblical standards which God Himself will empower us to fulfill?

How do we determine the difference between an act that is selfish, or selfless, or necessary to self-preservation? Which of these is always right? Or ever wrong?

What if our men disappoint us? How bad must they be before we desert them?

What if choices we made as young girls lead to dead-ends as adults? Are we imprisoned forever?

Counselors such as Dr. Lynn Jones Parker do not view women runaways as a problem. "I see it as a *solution* to a problem—domestic violence." The runaway is "one who is desperate and needs safety. . . . They are afraid for their children's lives, as well as for their own."[1]

This commonplace, tragic violation breeds complexities for family members and communities and churches and stirs a compassion all its own. We all know a story that fits this category. But our discussion of runaways ranges far beyond the monstrous scars of the battered woman.

A runaway, by this book's definition, abruptly abandons a social role. This leaves a social breach, a gaping wound, while she pursues growth or happiness or relief as an individual. It's difficult for the staid and steady members of the social order not to be outraged, shocked, and desperate to mend the fence. But how is that to be done?

Life in the past, until the 17th century, was lived in public . . . privacy scarcely ever existed when people lived on top of one another . . . to the extent that family privacy has increased, then, it is also likely that there has been a decrease in the social control and social support for the traditional definition of the performance of social roles.[2]

People today have more privacy and fewer controls from the outside than ever before. We also have fewer witnesses to daily travesties, less access to knowledge-able sympathizers, and less access to a more private world, the heart of the runaway. To feel beyond the act of betrayal and try to understand, we must listen to what she has to say in order to meet the needs of other hurting women around us. In order, perhaps, to understand ourselves.

If we are the bystanders who want to care, who want to be her friend, who want to be helpers, we need to deal with our own feelings and judgments. We must answer her critics, and now ours. After all, in reaching out to the runaway, do we condone the act?

The Christian who wants to come alongside the adult runaway may also face accusations—by unbe-lievers, of being out of step with our culture, of being more concerned with making the woman search her soul when she wants to gain the whole world instead; by other Christians, who caution us not to get emotionally involved, not to be unduly influenced by her thinking, but rather to stay within the guardrail of certain biblical standards.

What does it take to be an effective friend for a potential or actual runaway?

Profile of a Helper

God designed the church to be a caring community . . . We can't escape the fact that when we fail to bless

and love our brothers and sisters in Christ, we are failing in our duties as a family of God. When one member
of the body rejoices, we should all rejoice. When one
member weeps, we should all weep.[3]

We care, but we don't always know what to do. We
often lack knowledge of practical, wise ways to help
people in crises. The problems may seem beyond us,
by education or spiritual knowledge. But we don't have
to have all the answers, or any answers.

A wounded or harassed person usually wants to talk
about what's inside. We listen and care for "the needs of
those who are disoriented and despairing because of
the complexities of life, the injustices of others, or the
consequences of their own sin."[4]

We begin with emotional firstaid.

A Listening Heart

Sometimes a sufferer just needs relaxation, a listening Christian friend, or honest confession to a person
he has wronged. Prayer and supporting relationships
with other believers are vital.[5]

"We have lost the art of listening," Ruth says. "I think
we are still preaching to each other too much. When I
share prayer requests in a group, immediately I get
three responses. Someone will quote a Bible verse.
Another person will tell me how she handled a similar
situation, and a third person will dismiss my request by
saying that it's no big deal. All I want is for someone to
listen to me and pray with me."[6]

James 1:19 advises, "Be quick to listen, slow to
speak and slow to become angry."

She may not want advice. She's groaning through a
time of final resolve or confusion. She wants to spew out
what's inside. A listening heart can keep her going until
the fog clears, or the cavalry arrives.

Meanwhile, we try to see and feel and hear from her point of view.

Let her talk. Repeat to her what we think she's saying. Acknowledge that we hear her words and are trying to feel or understand her pain. Engage in active listening.

Active listening—avoiding the temptation to react with flippant platitudes or clucking disapproval.

Active listening—paying careful attention, assessing what is said and how, and what is not said; watching body language and including (mentally) other information we may have about the situation.

Active listening—taking time to perceive the social, physical, and emotional climate in which she existed, and the reasoning that led to running.

Active listening—asking probing questions, "How did that make you feel?" "What did you do then?" "How did he/she respond?" "What do you think should be done?"

Active listening—encouraging this friend to tell her side of the story, while always remembering this is only *one* side of the story.

Active listening—attempting to understand her problems and the methods she uses to handle them; discerning the right time to make suggestions or referrals.

Active listening—not monopolizing the conversation.

Active listening—absorbing details of her hellish hole and grasping the full impact of her enticements to run.

Active listening—discerning that what's being told must be kept confidential. Confidence, trust, are the essentials of a priceless friend.

We try to learn everything we can about her situation, while also being discerning. Some of what we think we know could be wrong.

Final judgments are reserved until we're able to hear the same scenarios from other participants. The story can seem so different when other details and perspectives are added. That doesn't mean we can't still care about the friend and her claims, but our input can be more objective and beneficial when we know the rest of the story.

What a gift from heaven, what an earthly treasure to find one other compatible human in whom we can confess our moods, our irritations, our desires, and our discomforts in the sweet sanctuary of friendship. May we all find that kind of kindred spirit in our own time of need, when we feel desperate to run away from it all. And may we all learn to become confidants with whom others can unload in safety and love.

Words of Hope and Healing

A listening ear and heart are therapeutic, but "a word aptly spoken is like apples of gold in settings of silver" (Proverbs 25:11).

There's nothing in the world like the wonder of the right word at the right time. Even well-placed humor can lighten the load of the depressed or desperate.

One day, Dr. Bernie S. Siegel, author of *Peace, Love and Healing*, got a call from a friend who is a police officer: "I have nothing to live for. I just called to say good-by because I'm going to commit suicide." Without a pause, Siegel quipped, "If you do, I'll never speak to you again." Astounded, the friend started to chuckle. Instead of shooting himself, he decided to go see Bernie for a heart-to-heart chat.[7]

When the time is right, we can speak words of encouragement, and even some of guidance. We no longer want her just to *feel* better, but to *get* better.

Encouragement—offering a practical plan of action and leaving it to the friend to follow through or not.

Encouragement—respecting any and all of her efforts to relieve her chaos.

Encouragement—agreeing on at least one step forward.

Encouragement—a blessing, a benediction, a helping hand.

Encouragement—asking oneself, *Is there any way I can identify? Have I ever done, felt, experienced something similar?*

Sometimes writing a letter, studying what we're thinking and feeling and wanting to say to her in recorded words ahead of time, allows us to carefully craft our message. Then we can set it aside for a few days before returning to it to assess the tone and choice of words. She'll have the privilege of responding privately first and the advantage of a permanent record to read over and over. Perhaps your concern and compassion, translated into writing, can penetrate at a deeper level.

"I try to get them to agree with the idea that if things are so awful, talking with someone can't make it any worse," one woman discovered. "That often makes sense and eases anxiety about opening up."[8]

A Calm, Cool Head

The foundation of discontent is so deep that no easy answer will prevail. It often goes back the distance to their own childhood . . . and they have to want help.[9]

The tough work of reconstruction comes when the listening and the encouraging have built a measure of trust. The central problem needs to be faced. There's a core issue somewhere surrounded by a complexity of causes and effects.

If our friend is a potential runaway, that is, she hasn't completely departed from the scene, we can nudge her to consider:

- all the pros and cons of this action
- who will benefit
- who will be most hurt
- her source of ultimate wisdom
- someone she should talk to first
- how long she can wait

If our friend has already run, we can be cautious about attaching blame; we can see her as a person with special needs, not as a problem.

Often, by the time a friend confides in us it's too late to reverse the course. Her mind's set. Her will's determined. She has or will run. She may be looking for a sounding board, or an advocate. She may come to you "looking for sanction . . . you need to be cautious . . . eventually she could put the blame on you."[10]

Rarely is there a blameless party in any broken relationship. And if the runaway harbors bitterness or animosity, reconciliation attempted too soon may not be healthy.

Personal Resources

> Brothers, if someone is caught in a sin, you who are spiritual should restore him gently. But watch yourself, or you also may be tempted. Carry each other's burdens, and in this way you will fulfill the law of Christ.
>
> Galatians 6:1–2

Macie is an at-home runaway. She walks around her house in a daze most the time. When her toddler needs attention, she puts him in bed. She doesn't cook, clean, or talk to her children. Her husband doesn't know what to do, so he takes the family out to eat or cooks meals himself. She's physically there, but mentally checked out.

Vivian is a potential runaway. She's been caring for her chronically ill child for thirteen years. Her husband operates his own business, and he can't take time off to help in crises. Vivian drives her son to endless tests and treatments, but there's no cure in sight. In spite of her consuming efforts, he will probably die before he's grown.

Vivian thinks of running away because she can't fix things for him and because she doesn't want to watch him die. She feels responsible, that she must do it all. Meanwhile, she refuses offers of help. "We're okay," she insists, "We always manage somehow."

If we know a woman who has a load that seems heavy, it probably is. If we find ourselves saying, "I don't know how she manages from day to day," there's probably a great need.

One author writes, "Those of us who look the toughest are often the most fragile."[11]

But how much time and energy and emotion can we give to this special need? How high a priority should this woman's life and problems and complications be given?

Can we be committed to her, no matter what? Is our empathy dependent upon who is the bad guy or good guy? Or is it dependent upon how much time and energy all this is going to take? Her misplaced confidence in us can lead to more trouble and even disaster. The pain's still there. The going's much slower. No one's been helped.

"Like a bad tooth or a lame foot is reliance on the unfaithful in times of trouble" (Proverbs 25:19).

What does the woman need most right now?

Does she need medical attention? Would she appreciate lunch out with a friend? Can you offer her a coffee or tea break? Does she need child care? Does she need someone to help with housework? Does she need professional counseling? Does she need a place of safety, a refuge? Does she need a meal? Can you make some phone calls or run some errands? Who can best help her? And what is your part in it?

This kind of friendship takes time—regular contact through steady phone calls, visits, sending cards, running errands, constant prayer. We must be on a similar schedule, a complementary track.

Elaine Nelson Thompson moved to another state and a woman in her new community invited her to church. "When I could think of no more excuses, I cautiously attended services. After a few months a woman in the church called me and invited me to her home. 'I want to talk to you about something,' she said."

"I agonized all night. What had she heard about me? Was she going to tell me I was no longer welcome in her fellowship? Was my past to forever plague me?"

"What a wonderful relief to discover she needed a prayer partner. She wanted to know if I'd meet with her on a regular basis. Over the months we prayed and shared and I dared hope I'd finally found a kindred spirit who would support me as I walked through a replay of all the things I'd done and had been done to me. Soon I began to search for avenues of restitution and entered ministry service again."[12]

A friend from the sidelines is one thing, but inviting an adult runaway into our homes is a major commitment that must be carefully considered. What is best for her in the long run? How long can she stay? Do we know enough about her situation to feel comfortable with this offer? Can our family absorb the impact? Is this a wise course? Is there a better alternative?

Rhoda shared her experience. "As her neighbor I could see Coleen's need to get away from her abusive boyfriend. So, when she ran to my house one night with her two children, I didn't hesitate to allow her to take refuge. However, within moments her boyfriend was at our door, threatening us all with a gun. I wanted to call the police. She begged me to wait. While he pounded on our door, I pulled her son away from my daughter when he threatened her with a pool stick. I felt suddenly trapped in my own home."

Her problems may seem never-ending. She may not be a quick fix. How much of our lives are we prepared to give to her and her needs?

Befriending a potential or actual runaway is best suited to those who have spiritual gifts of wisdom, discernment, service and helps, or encouragement (see Romans 12, 1 Corinthians 12) and the character traits of tough love, endurance, and perseverance (Romans 5:3–5; 2 Thessalonians 3:5). Is it possible to join with several others who have gifts of listening and counsel, who can keep our get-togethers private among themselves, who can support us in our efforts to be a confidential friend and guide us through the complications? For instance, a fine line at times exists between helping, and aiding and abetting.

Maria, widowed and unable to care for her children in Honduras, left them with her mother and migrated to the U.S. in search of a job. After working several years, she fell in love, married, and started a new family. However, she was homesick for her growing children back home. A church learned of her desire to see her kids. They raised money for a plane ticket so that she could visit her homeland, and she left. She called one day, six months later, to explain, "They don't want to come to the strange land and I want to stay here with them." Her American husband and baby never saw her again. The members of the church found themselves in the awkward position of being party to splitting a family, enabling a runaway.

Professional Referrals

When should a Christian seek professional help to solve an emotional problem? When the problem is long-term, recurrent, or debilitating.[13]

Professional help is needed if we can answer yes to any of these questions:
- Is she addicted to drugs or alcohol?
- Is she debilitated by physical, emotional, or sexual abuse?
- Is she severely depressed?
- Is she seriously ill?
- Is she suicidal?

Stepping Aside

Can we release her?

Sometimes we must back off, or step away completely. Can we sense the right time and method? Our purpose in this friend's life may come to a close. Perhaps she needs others.

Are we willing to set her free from our control? Are we willing to relinquish our privileged but temporary role? Can we remain thankful for our part in her life, and now get on with our own?

We may discover she has other listening friends and we chafe under the perceived competition for her confidences. We thought she was our exclusive ministry property, our private project. We must release her from the pride of possessiveness.

As a rule, the best nurture for a woman in crisis is building a support network, a community of nurturers, exhorters, and encouragers.

Release her—when we've given everything we've got and she shows no progress, or pays no attention to our pearls of wisdom.

Release her—when we thought we knew her: her thoughts, her intentions, her need to run once. And then, she runs again.

Release her—when the ship's about to sink and you both realize that God is doing His own work (see Jonah 1:4–12).

Release her—trust God to protect her, to discipline and teach her, even if she remains a prodigal.

Release her—until she's cured of her waywardness, until she finally finds *home*. Until she becomes "wiser, though torn!"[14]

Release her—but still offer love and friendship.

The Power of Touch

Touch is far more essential than our other senses. In describing final departures, we often talk of "losing touch" . . . . Among other things, touch teaches us the difference between *I* and *other*, that there can be someone outside of ourselves.[15]

A hug. A pat on the shoulder. A kiss on the cheek. A clutch of the hand. One more way of showing support and meeting a very human need. This is crucial especially if she's opened up a harrowing experience or confessed an ugly side of herself and wonders if we'll turn away.

Most runaways, separated from those who should be loving her, long for affection.

The Spiritual Side of Running Away

Prayer

Most every human problem has a spiritual solution. Prayer frees the mind and will, steadies the emotions and affections, stunts the influence of evil, and opens the windows of heaven. A friend in crisis needs a prayer partner more than anything else.

We must pray before we meet together.

We must pray while we're visiting, both silently to ourselves and aloud if she's willing.

We must pray after we've had contact, for ourselves as well as our friend.

Ask of Him as many 'what' questions as 'why' pleas. "What do you want us to learn, Lord?" "What do you want us to do?"

When she's ready, we can intercede with her on behalf of those who have hurt her, and for those whom she has caused pain.

God can enlighten us with insights no one knows but Him, perhaps not even the runaway. The supernatural, divine element in our interchanges will accomplish spiritual purposes, will encourage us with the revelation, "God is here with us! He cares! He will carry us through."

The goal is to pray for miracles while accepting freedom of choice.

Confrontation and Grace

The knowledge that "something is not right within" affects the moods of the self, muddles the motives, and constantly reminds us that we are not at our best . . . the deep discontent and discord within . . . a basic perversion has blighted us.[16]

We can safely generalize and assume that one of the reasons she ran had something to do with sin—her own and/or someone else's. Sin destroys relationships. Sin distorts values. Sin mixes motives. Sin separates friends and family. Sin deceives. Sin is universal.

But what sin, exactly? And how can it be reversed? These questions should be carefully weighed in the court of time and spiritual discernment.

The runaway desperately needs a friend to help her "cross bridges of insight and understanding," before she "can begin to face responsibility and accountability to God."[17] Her storm needs to be stilled.

She may have a critical moral dilemma to face. For instance, if her need or desire to run contradicts a standard she has held as an absolute: she's dying inside a destructive relationship, yet struggles with the vow she made "till death do us part."

John Thompson explains the struggle he had. "In the three years before the divorce I produced a number of successful contemporary Christian albums. But after the divorce, I canceled the ones I was scheduled to work on and basically walked away from the whole business."

"I was living with such guilt because of my failed marriage that I felt staying in the Christian music industry put me into a hypocritical life confusion."

In that same mode of thinking, he borrowed financial problems too. "For the next years I lived in a state of confusion. I chose what to call totally wrong. I chose what to rationalize as a weakness of someone with 'an artistic temperament.' So for the next six years I continued to neglect many of my financial obligations. I was being 'artistic.' "[18]

We must study the whole counsel of God and seek insight from mature Christians to determine the spirit, as well as the letter, of the law.

> Grace demands that we apply biblical requirements with tender compassion. Grace seeks to help. Grace is remedial. It seeks to resolve conflicts and replace pain with peace.[19]

Questions to consider—first in solitude, and then together with our friend:
- What decisions has she already made?
- What actions have already been taken?
- What are her most crucial challenges?
- To whom, or to what, is she committed?
- How would Jesus relate to this woman?
- What Christian values relate to her case?

- What laws of God has she broken?
- What do you believe to be God's will for her?
- What are some facts, and some principles, with which we both can agree?
- What is her relationship with God? With Jesus Christ?
- What's her view of the Bible?

"My life is so unfair," the runaway laments out of her anguish. Her words may be hostile, exaggerated, perhaps even untrue or blasphemous. However, she needs a podium and an audience.

"Come now, let us reason together," says the Lord, as He begins His case against the sin of Judah (Isaiah 1:18).

Each of us strives to discover the meaning of our existence. In the process, we approach our Creator and heavenly Father either as a foe or friend. For some, this comes while working through their distresses, or railing against their circumstances. It comes when they feel like running away.

Discovery Questions

1. Christian psychologist Larry Crabb, one of the pioneers in the field, proposes that lay counseling should take place on three levels.

Level One is counseling by encouragement. All members of a local church should learn to be caring, sensitive people who show support and loving concern for both Christians and nonbelievers.

Level Two is counseling by exhortation. This is a more in-depth type of helping. It is done by mature believers who have learned basic counseling skills in a training program.

Level Three is counseling by enlightenment. A few selected members in each local church take more advanced training for a six-to-twelve month period. The trainees learn how to handle deeper, more stubborn problems that rarely yield to encouragement or exhortation.[20]

At which of these levels are you?

At which of these levels would you like to be and why?

What must you do to accomplish this?

If you have a runaway friend, which one of these types of counselors does she need most right now?

2. What are your strengths as a friend of a runaway? What are your weaknesses?

3. What is God's view of a runaway? List examples or verses from Scripture.

4. Study Galatians 6:1–2.
    What is to be the condition and attitude of the helper, according to these verses? What is the warning, and why do you think it was given?

5. What are the dangers of shelters and halfway houses for women wanting to run? How could they be most helpful? How could women's groups or churches get involved? What would be some practical and wise goals?

Notes

[1]Parker, letter.

[2]Gove, Style, and Hughes, "Effect of Marriage," 17.

[3]Gary Smalley and John Trent, *The Blessing* (New York: Simon & Schuster, Pocket Books, 1986), 201.

[4]Joseph M. Stowell, "A Multitude of Counselors," *Moody*, May 1991, 4.

[5]Susan Harrington, "When Emotional Hurts Need an Expert's Help," *Moody*, November 1982, 43.

[6]Becky Durost Fish, "Caught between Expectations," *Moody*, February 1992, 15.

[7]Sue Browder, "How to Build Better Friendships," *Reader's Digest*, March 1990, 58.

[8]Collister, letter.

[9]Bogle, letter.

[10]Ibid.

[11]Gloria Chisholm, *The Secret of the Swan* (Minneapolis: Augsburg, 1993), 107.

[12]E. N. Thompson, interview.

[13]Harrington, "Emotional Hurts," 44.

[14]Ruth Bell Graham, *Prodigals and Those Who Love Them* (Colorado Springs: Focus on the Family, 1991), 15,

[15]Diane Ackerman, "The Power of Touch," *Parade*, 25 March 1990, 5.

[16]James Earl Massey, *The Soul Under Siege* (Grand Rapids: Francis Asbury Press, 1987), 19–20.

[17]Stowell, "A Multitude of Counselors," 4.

[18]John Thompson and Patti Thompson, *Dance of the Broken Heart* (Nashville: Abingdon, 1986), 109.

[19]Stowell, "The Divorce Dilemma," *Moody*, November 1991, 15.

[20]Lawrence J. Crabb, Jr., *Effective Biblical Counseling* (Grand Rapids: Zondervan, 1977), 190.

Five

Dangers, Toils, and Snares
Befriending a Runaway:
Part Two

"We reached out to our daughter-in-law the best we knew how when she left our son and the kids," one woman sighs. "We see her on occasion, but she acts as if nothing's changed. She's never opened up to us, though we have the main care of her children now. We're struggling to overcome the anger and frustration."

Genevieve and her family pursued Mary Ellen, another runaway. They wanted to assure her of their continued love and concern for her and her choices when she checked out overnight from her job, her family, her friends. They tracked down her new address, wrote her notes, and called her several times a week, to find out what she was doing and to keep her posted on happenings in her former community.

Meanwhile, they also extended support to Mary Ellen's deserted parents and friends, trying to walk through this rejection with them. "We wanted to try to leave the door open on both sides, in case she changed her mind and wanted to return," Genevieve explains. "But she never responded."

In another case, an employer tried to approach an assistant about troubling signs of withdrawal and moodiness. "She got very upset and accused me of harassing her. She was polite after that, but we didn't share together. I knew she was experiencing stress at home and I wanted to help. One day she didn't show up and I still can't get over my sense of failure."

We can't always get it right, every time. We're flawed humans who try to make others perfect. We're blind, but we try to speak. We're deaf, but we try to see. We should be silent, but we try to get through with our muffled messages. Our goal should be to learn how to "love each other deeply, because love covers over a multitude of sins" (1 Peter 4:8).

"No! You have everything wrong! That's not the way it is with me," a runaway friend may accuse, if she speaks to us at all.

"You don't understand me. You don't even try!" she yells, flatly denying our interpretation of her life.

"Why do you insist it's my fault? Don't you listen? Can't you see anything from my side?" she cries, when we touch some hidden nerve.

"You think everything's black or white, all right or all wrong. Can't you feel my pain? Don't you see it's not working for me? It's easy for you in your comfortable world."

What do we do when it seems we're talking to ourselves, when we sense the gloom of failure? We know our motives, or we think we do. We know what we're thinking, or what we meant to say. But there's a one-way communication with a major gap between.

More Things to Watch for

Elaine Nelson Thompson explains one reason why it can be so difficult for the runaway to allow anyone close to her. "I started going to church again and an elderly woman took me under her wing. I slowly began to come out of my shell. Then, one day, the woman pulled me aside. 'We just learned you are divorced and would prefer you not come here anymore.' I was crushed, devastated. After that it was hard for me to get involved in a church fellowship, much less draw close to any of the members."[1]

Many runaways are extremely sensitive to judgment. She may slant our well-meaning words with a harsh and condemning edge because of past blows. We have one perception of how we believe we're helping our friend, and then there's the way she's actually receiving it. Did we miscue?

Then again, it's possible that we've spoken and acted appropriately, that we've shown love in all its fullness, and she still misunderstands.

Or we may realize that she's advancing an agenda of her own, building a case for her side in a revenge game. Are we being used? Or lied to?

The Sting of Honesty

"If it were I, I would appeal to God; I would lay my cause before him," said Eliphaz to his friend Job, who suffered boils and humiliations on a dung heap (Job 5:8).

Self-righteous—that's how we sound when we plead our case to those who run. Job's friends mixed their advice with bits of truth and misunderstanding and emotional prejudice, all on behalf of God. Job sensed his friends weren't on his side. They seemed to want to slap him, to kick him, when he was already down. They spoke truth, but too soon, with a sting that brought infection, not healing.

They quarreled with him out of misunderstanding. They hadn't run in his shoes, nor felt his pain.

They were steeped in emotional prejudice. "There you are in your fix, and here I am in my cozy corner. Job, obviously you did something dreadfully wrong!"

They were dripping with pious pleas. They knew God and His ways and His standards and His commands. They certainly knew why Job was suffering.

"In my case, if a friend says something a little critical," one woman admits, "I can take it. But if my sister says the exact same words, I'm livid."

Do we have a rapport with the runaway? Or do we irritate one another, becoming part of the problem rather than the solution?

The Lash of Anger

People in crisis can be edgy, even hostile.

A runaway woman may vent her steam on us. She may accuse us of neglect, of not coming forward sooner when she was struggling in private. She may not believe we could possibly understand. She may resent our own happier circumstances. She may fear or resent our attempts to convince her to return.

Candy finally admitted she couldn't stand to be with her husband, Tom, anymore. She detailed his many offenses and then concluded, "What do you think I should do?"

Her friend asked questions, trying to see the whole situation, then suggested, "How about a marriage counselor?"

Candy stormed into the kitchen and slammed some cupboard doors. "Oh, sure. Weeks, months, maybe years, spilling our hearts out to a stranger. Tom will never be different. Meanwhile, my life is slipping away. Bryan has helped me to see that so clearly."

"Bryan? Is he a counselor?"

"No!" she said, still fuming. "He's a friend. The only close male friend I've ever had. Tom can never measure up. Bryan's all I ever wanted in a man."

Candy was angry because her friend didn't show pity during her long diatribe of Tom's failures. She had already made up her mind, and she didn't want it changed.

At times we may want to shake our friend, or scream at her. Other moments we'll long to wrap her in our arms and weep. We'll want to cry out with the psalmist, "Save us and help us with your right hand, that those you love may be delivered" (Psalm 60:5).

A Crime? A Family Member?

When the runaway confides that violence by a family member caused her to run, the helper's role is complicated—by embarrassment, and possibly fear, if we know the abuser. And by moral and legal issues, if the perpetrator is unknown to us.

Should the crime be reported? To whom? Should the alleged abuser be confronted? What kind of protection can be provided? Will the victim be believed? Should the family be kept together at all costs, even in a deadly home environment?

Helpers of runaways in domestic violence cases should act with great care in thinking about and finding options.

> Anything that helps someone find safety, and (helps) them find out that the church cares . . . is a huge step toward their healing.[2]

Helping Others Without Hurting Ourselves

Above all else, guard your heart, for it is the wellspring of life.

Proverbs 4:23

Warning: helping a friend in need can be dangerous to one's own health and happiness.

Reaching out in empathy underscores some of the discontent we harbor. Some of her complaints, frustrations, or wounds are our own. As we empathize and commiserate with knowing nods and shared tears, she may look into our eyes and say, "Wanna run away with me?"

Waltzing a hurting female into our arena opens emotional bonding potentials for other members of our families, including our husbands. Rocky marriages are especially vulnerable. However, even contented couples can be shaken by the close proximity of intriguing victims who hang onto our every word and deed.

Helpers of friends in crisis need ways to handle the stress while the friend is stressed. We need backup emotional support and sometimes we need chaperons. Good diet, some exercise, a full night's rest, keeping our hands and feet busy will help balance our minds and bodies and keeps pushing us forward to positive resolution.

There are times when an encourager needs to be encouraged. If the friend's choice to run produces nothing but vengeance, slander, and devastation, she'll want to cling like a drowning victim to anyone with a sign of compassion. Both may feel they're going under with the struggle. There will be moments of regret for willingness to take an active part as the emotional repercussions from her decision spill over to those who reach out.

But true love is difficult to show from a distance. Close and committed contact, kept in healthy balance, provides the key for timely action. We're there when she needs us. We're there when the breakthrough comes. We've survived the traumatic nights and storms and can now prove we're more than blustery words on a spring day. A friend of a runaway takes her hand and walks her the long way home.

Watch for Feelings

> Knowledge of one's own human condition is the key to having compassion for others.[3]

How do we really feel? About the runaway? About the others affected by her running?

People who have the hardest time with compassion for a runaway are those who feel a woman should stay in her appointed station—no matter what; those who haven't heard her whole story; those who minister to the abandoned ones left behind. People who are in difficult situations themselves but toughing it out and not liking it, who have been used or lied to before, those who are part of the Cynical Samaritan Syndrome.

On the other hand, those who may find it easiest to empathize and reach out to women who run are ones who believe that any woman who seeks any kind of change is exercising her rights as a female, who only think of domestic violence issues when they hear a woman has run away, who have practical helps, skills, or training to share that will help her back on her feet, who understand the grace of God and His heart for all runaways.

It's not always easy to assess our own motives in wanting to help a runaway. We may see ourselves as performing an act of kindness and decency when, in fact, we may be vicariously acting out our own penchant for running away. Perhaps the helper has suffered silently under abusive parents or an oppressive spouse or feels like a failure in other life choices. Some clues could be eagerness to believe the worst about those left behind—perceiving them as the enemy, unwilling to urge the runaway to consider restoration of relationships, unable to keep confidences, keeping the runaway stirred up emotionally—either in anger or self-pity—and those who are unwilling to allow the runaway to grow in perspective or insight.

Emotional prejudice is best judged by outsiders. Others may say things like, "Hey, watch it! You're getting too involved here." "She can do no wrong in your eyes." "She has you wrapped up and hog-tied." "You never talk about anything or anyone else anymore."

Did She Really Run Away?

Friends or family members may label as running away an act the woman sincerely considered to be finding where she belongs.

"It can be frustrating to try to be what other people want you to be instead of what you know is right for you," Julie tries to explain. Her peers and relatives and colleagues see her as disgruntled and hard to please, unable to settle down as she runs from company to company in pursuit of a perfect job.

"People measure success differently," she says simply. She wants a job that uses her education and skills, but also isn't "at odds with her faith." But all anyone else can see are all the dream jobs she leaves behind.[4]

A woman may seem to be running from a relationship when she's just needing some space. Bette Jane has a habit of disappearing from view when she's in a melancholy mood. "I don't want to talk to anyone during those periods. I need to think, to reflect about what I'm feeling and why. It's important that I have some privacy, some time to myself. My friends think I'm upset with them. It usually has nothing to do with them."

Another woman put it this way: "Everyone I knew was running, running all the time. It's like Lewis Carroll said, we had to run just to keep in the same place. If we wanted to change course, we had to run twice as fast. I wanted to scream, 'Stop! Time out! Where am I going? What am I doing?' The irony to me was that when I finally did step aside for a break, I was the one accused of running away."

Lessons From the Runaway

What is she teaching me? What am I learning from her experience? The time we've spent in worry and prayer and success and failure doesn't have to go to waste. Her very needs may be the opportunities for God to stretch us, train us for assignments He's preparing ahead. We can embrace her purpose in this season of our lives.

> Learning more about the people who feel compelled to leave their surroundings in such an unorthodox manner, and about the spouses or parents or children they left behind, may illuminate aspects of our own lives and the lives of persons dear to us.[5]

Watch for Turning Points

Watch for a change in her attitude that signifies she's seeing her situation from a larger viewing screen. Perhaps she's gained hope. Or she's getting serious about overcoming an addiction. Or she's facing hard facts about herself. Or she's experiencing a spiritual conversion.

At these junctures she doesn't need us to soften the blows of reality nor to deliver the final punch. She needs us to come alongside and help her navigate the bends in the road. She will benefit from our encouragement to face not only what she was in the past, but who she is now and what she can become.

The Ultimate Runaway

Barbie came home on medical leave from her job overseas to live with her sister, Karen, and Karen's family. She said she'd been suffering from depression. Never married, forty-two years old, as high in her profession as she could go, she seemed to have it all.

"She had been with us four months. Everything seemed fine," Karen reported. She was looking forward to getting back to her job. She loved going to my kids' school and sports activities. We had a game scheduled that night. But she called me at work, doped and spacey.

I called 911 and rushed home. She was sprawled on the floor. She had taken a full bottle of antidepressants and tranquilizers and slit her wrists."

Karen was totally disillusioned. "We tried to give her help. We tried to give her hope. We wanted so much to be part of her healing. Where did we fail?"

Mental disease and alcohol or drug abuse are the main contributing factors to suicide. Other factors include "isolation, a lack of involvement with significant others, impulsiveness and feelings of rage, helplessness, and hopelessness." It's stress on top of a reduced ability to cope with stress.[6]

The Ironies of Freedom

> The negative side of freedom, the burden which it puts upon man, is difficult to realize, especially for those whose heart is with the cause of freedom.[7]

When one thing is gained, another can be lost. Getting rid of one evil can usher in new and more besetting restraints. Outer freedom can't guarantee control of inner enemies: compulsions, fears, and false perceptions. As one runaway said, "I know exactly what I left behind, but I don't know what I'm going to."

It's like the short-lived joy of celebration on the face of a prisoner who has labored to dig himself out under the thick walls of his prison only to discover his hole breaks through on top a railroad track—and a train is barreling down just a few feet away.

At the same time that the runaway becomes more independent and self-reliant she can also become more isolated, alone, and fearful. Freedom can intensify insecurities. Freedom may drive a runaway to give blind devotion to someone who seems to have the answers to her life. Though she's anxious about what to do next, she may not be willing to go back to where she was. She may feel powerless and, therefore, vulnerable.

"If you succeed in becoming more independent," explains psychologist Sonya Friedman, author of *Smart Cookies Don't Crumble,* "others may view you as being able to take care of yourself, in which case they may be freer to leave you or to expect more of you."[8]

Has she fled from one bondage only to find another?

What moral principles are guiding her?

What will she have at the end of this journey?

Has she found negative or positive freedom? Freedom *from* what? Freedom *to do* what? Is she able to pursue some constructive goal? Can she give herself to some work or a relationship that's emotionally, mentally, spiritually, or physically healthy? Or is cessation of stress all she gained, with no other progress in sight?

The Heart of a Runaway

I loathe my very life;
therefore I will give free rein
to my complaint
and speak out in the bitterness
of my soul.

Job 10:1

Actual and potential adult runaways are impossible to lump into neat categories. Each one is a special set of needs and dynamics. Some are very responsible, conscientious, and caring. Most have become isolated in some way.

She wants the liberty to do something or be someone. Or she wants the liberty from a place, a situation, a person.

[There is] the need to be related to the world outside oneself, the need to avoid aloneness. To feel completely alone and isolated leads to mental disintegration just as physical starvation leads to death.[9]

Most humans have a need to relate to others, to have a feeling of community, a sense of belonging. In one survey of twenty thousand readers of *Cosmopolitan* magazine, respondents revealed the number one need of a woman in marriage is "basic emotional connection between husband and wife." Emotional abuse was listed as the single biggest reason for wanting a divorce.[10] What powerful emotional needs are pulling her away, causing her to run?

Did she run out of fear? Then she needs security, safety, assurance, courage. We need to help her discern between real and imagined fears and find some kind of overcoming strategy.

Did she run out of hopelessness? Then she needs encouragement, a stirring of faith, the practice of gratitude, a mind and heart enlarged to see broader vistas, to understand deeper truths. She needs a purpose, a grasp of what her life can mean, some worthy goals. She needs to mark a path through her struggles, conflicts and sorrows.

Did she run out of rebellion? Then she needs reproof from someone she knows truly loves and cares for her, who can turn "the rock into a pool, the hard rock into springs of water" (Psalm 114:8). We may need to leave her to roam her world until she finds repentance or some cause higher then herself to which she can cling.

Did she run to seek adventure? Then she needs to understand the risks of leaving the predictable and learn discernment until "wisdom will enter [her] heart, and knowledge will be pleasant to [her] soul" (Proverbs 2:10). Different sights, fresh sounds, divine appointments may give her understanding of the old life or help her forge a new one.

Did she run after love? Then she needs to feel loved—for someone close to her to learn her love language, to communicate through words or touch or time spent or deeds or thoughtful gifts. She needs to learn how to go looking for love in all the right places.

Did she run because she's addicted to running? Then she needs deliverance—when she's at the end of herself, and wants help, and is willing to submit to the treatment that will calm down her agitation that tells her she has to keep moving. She needs connections to people and a place where she can practice the art of commitment. She needs to pull away from the ranks of drifters who move from town to town, job to job, tied to no one and no longer knowing who they are.

Did she run for her sake, or for the sake of others? Running away can be a stab at some kind of justice—to escape unfairness, to retaliate for a wrong, to force a change, to flee from an evil.

Or it can be a woman's last ditch effort to finally "do something for myself."

Did she run to leave a place where she feels she doesn't belong?

> Chicago police call them "wanderers," "walkers," or "repeaters." They are old people—some depressed, some senile, some merely looking for action—who stray from nursing and rest homes . . . [they are] often loners who cannot handle institutional living.[11]

There are others who discover, too late, they don't easily manage family living.

Rona's a potential runaway. Never married before, at age thirty-five she married into a family with three girls, ages twelve to seventeen. "I love my husband very much, but the hostility from the stepkids is killing me. The constant, daily lack of respect and the fights and the nonsupport of discipline from their dad are dividing us. Sometimes the stress is so great, I want to take him away, and leave the girls behind."

Did she run as some kind of social statement? A rebel with a cause, she has something to prove: careers before kindred, independence over submission, rising above the crowd instead of community. She's probably troubled by those who tell her to recognize her place and not aspire to anything more. She's driven by important needs of her own to find herself as a person.

The Philosophy of Running

Should we seek what's best for this one woman? Or what's best for her family? Or the community at large? Or what pleases God? Must there be winners and losers, or is there one solution that incorporates all the needs?

Are those who run the courageous ones? Or is courage born through the daily plod of contenting one's self with choices made, buckling under one's lot in life, submitting to various disciplines? Is it easier to give in or to fight?

But if a woman willingly and cheerfully chooses to remain in her place, isn't that a kind of freedom? Isn't she by this act developing into a free, self-determining, productive individual?

Our answers to these questions will be largely determined by how we think about the following:

- For whom should we live?
- Is this earthly existence all there is?
- What is the purpose of life?

Discovery Questions

1. The following is a proposed Bill of Rights for adult runaways. Study it and consider: Should a runaway have any such rights at all? What would you change about this list of rights? Which item on this list means the most to you and why?

Rights of a Runaway
or
Ten Commandments for Friends of a Runaway

   1. Give her the benefit of the doubt—assume she had compelling reasons.

   2. Tell her what effect her running away has had on significant people.

   3. Assure her of the unconditional love of God.

   4. Let her know you're one caring person who misses her and wants her back.

   5. Tell her the truth—that because of her action, some things have forever been lost.

   6. Encourage her with tales of positive changes that have been made.

   7. Allow her to ask uncomfortable questions.

   8. Help her assess the pros and cons of returning, and not returning.

   9. Respect her free will.

10. Pray her to her home.

2. Author Kay Strom says, "Although it doesn't take an expert to be an effective people helper, not everyone can be one. Real helpers need to have certain Here-am-I-Lord-use-me characteristics." She prepared a list of questions to aid in determining those with true helping abilities. If you can answer yes to these questions, God can use you.

• Do I have an honest concern for people who are hurting?

• Do I believe that God has the power to heal, however deep the hurt?

• Do I believe God can forgive, however great the sin?

• Am I willing to do whatever I can to help a hurting person?

• Am I willing to gain some basic knowledge of common crisis situations, of what to say and what not to say, of organizations and professionals to whom I can refer people for help?

• Can I recognize and accept my own limitations?[12]

3. The following bits of conversations are taken from actual or potential runaways. Mark with an *X* those statements that could have come from your own mouth at one time or another. Mark with an *O* those words you've heard a friend say.

"I'll meet a guy who's caring and sensitive and works for a decent wage. He'll take care of me and love me and I'll never be lonely again."

"I'll find a commune or shack someplace where I can rest and heal and find myself again."

"They'll be so shook up when they find I really left that they'll do anything to get me back. Then everything'll be perfect, or at least tolerable."

"I've changed and my family hasn't. I want a very spiritual life, but everything in my home is antispiritual. I try—I go to conferences and read books and learn some things to do, but nothing works. In fact, it gets worse. They're more antagonistic than ever."

"I'll rent a small studio and do nothing but paint—no kids, no busybodies, no meals to fix. Then I'll know if I really have the talent."

"I'll go to California (or is it Florida?) and mix with important people. Sooner or later something big will happen."

"I'll get a job, a real job. I'll make something of myself and then they'll be sorry how they treated me."

"I don't want to try anymore. People are a pain. If they'd just leave me alone I could take care of myself."

"I don't like staying long in any one place. I just earn enough money to get back on the road. I'm not happy unless I'm in perpetual motion—don't try to tie me down!"

"I don't know what I want or who I am. I really don't know what's wrong with me. Just let me sleep. Let me dream. Let me run away."

4. Read Job 19:13–22, the epitome of despair. Do you know anyone who ever felt this way? How did you view this person? What did you do?

5. Were you encouraged or discouraged by the chapters you've read so far in your desires to reach out as a helping friend to a runaway? Give specific examples.

Notes

[1]E. N. Thompson, interview.

[2]Jeaneen Watkins, "Silent Screams," by Linda Midgett, *Christianity Today,* 19 July 1993, 47.

[3]Robert S. McGee, *The Search for Freedom* (Ann Arbor, Mich., Servant, 1995), 17.

[4]Holly G. Miller, "Talkin' 'Bout My Generation," *Today's Christian Woman,* January/February 1995, 60.

[5]Brenton, "The Runaways," 17.

[6]Alan Berman, "Idaho Suicide Rate 30% Above National Average," interview by Associated Press, *Lewiston* (Idaho) *Morning Tribune,* 18 April 1995, A1.

[7]Fromm, *Escape from Freedom,* 104.

[8]Sonya Friedman, interview by Alice Kosner, "Making the Best of Change," *Cosmopolitan,* February 1992, 68.

[9]Fromm, *Escape from Freedom,* 19.

[10]Claudia Bowe, "Everything We Think, Feel, and Do about Divorce," *Cosmopolitan,* February 1992, 68.

[11]John Leo, quoted by Patricia Delaney, in "The New Runaways: Old Folks," *Time,* 13 July 1981, 57.

[12]Kay Marshall Strom, *Helping Women in Crisis* (Grand Rapids: Zondervan, 1986), 9.

Six

Mopping up the Mess

When a woman runs
a crag from hell falls
upon the unsuspecting.

Ten million dollars: what would that amount be worth to you? That's what surveyors asked adults, as reported in *The Day America Told the Truth*.

One in four respondents said, "I'd abandon my entire family."

Twenty three percent replied, "I'd become a prostitute for a week."

Sixteen percent insisted, "I'd be willing to leave my husband [or wife]."

Three percent would put their children up for adoption.[1]

A potential runaway is anyone who has a price.

Society tells us we have rights and expectations
and we need to take control and discover ourselves . . .
at any cost. Some women buy the idea . . . and forget
the cost.[2]

Commented one husband of a runaway, "Something was unleashed here that will plague us the rest of our lives. Something is lost that can never be regained."

The debris of the storm left behind is all we see for a time—the wounded casualties, the collateral damage, the third-party innocents, the entrenching of another social ill. Running always has a price tag.

> I never saw my father, and he became just a name on my birth certificate. My mother sent me to live with her parents, and she became the glamorous lady who breezed in for short visits. She would hold me, hug me, call me "baby," and then leave again.
>
> By the time I married, I was so full of hurt and bitterness that my self-image had hit zero. My husband, Dennis, said he loved me. But how could I believe him? My mother didn't love me. I didn't love myself. How could he love me? . . . As I experienced motherhood, it became harder to understand why my mother had abandoned me. As I held my pain and feelings of rejection closer, God seemed far away. I kept asking: He's a holy God; how could He love me?[3]

A break can mean something positive . . . or negative. It can produce good, or evil. A break can mean something's irreparably broken, or it can be a sudden open door. It can be a collapsing, a crumbling, a violation, or a breach. It can be a last chance, a fond hope realized, or an answered prayer. A runaway risks the consequences, which way her break will go, which way the results will flow—both for herself and the lives her action penetrates.

Someone needs to assess the immediate and long-range fallout to those caught in the whirlwind stirred by a run.

Withholding the gift of one's self

Old photos, few and precious, bits of conversations, wisp of a remembered scent, a longing for what might have been and what, perhaps, might still be—that's all that remains for many who have been left behind, the deserted ones. Relationships become frozen because contact is rare or nonexistent.

The daily building of memories; the comfort of touch; the companionship in sadness and glad times and just okay moments; to talk, to listen, to care, to relieve pent-up pressures; to work through the mass of problems. All the little details of human contact that encourage one to plod on in this earthly toil—these interchanges are stolen away, ripped apart, forever denied by the one who ran.

An abandoned father and husband pours out the pain of loneliness and rejection: "She left three days after we celebrated our fifteenth anniversary. I've had this empty feeling in my gut so long, I can't believe I'll ever be rid of it. Even simple things like joy and laughter seem an impossible dream, a fantasy from another world. The empty place beside me at night . . . no more meals on the table when I return home . . . no conversations about problems at work or with the kids . . . no more touching . . . . When I think back, I know she was trying to tell me. She'd let things go for a long time, then explode at me about the ways I needed to change. I tried. I really did. But it was never enough. I just never guessed she hated it here that much!"

Another suddenly single says, "How can I enjoy coming home to an empty house, not being needed, no one to take care of, no one to share life with? I feel as though I've been amputated, without my prior permission or knowledge."

When an adult leaves there's "a sudden reconfiguration of the family."[4]

It's been that way from the beginning.

Lucifer ran from God's rule and a cosmic war exploded.

Eve bit into his logic and had to run to the trees to hide. Her act opened the door for murder and mayhem and losing it all for her husband and sons and each of us, the children of Eve to come.

Who Will Take Care of the Kids?

Many suffer when women run—boyfriends, hus-bands, parents, friends, siblings, colleagues, relatives—but most of our attention will be given to the effects on children. These can be the children or grandchildren, nieces and nephews of the runaway, or any adolescents close enough to feel the impact of the rejection.

Even so, many of the same feelings and stages and responses can be felt by the adults in the runaway's path of departure. And they have the same needs for caring friends to help them work through their loss and disillusionment and feelings of blame.

Generational Fallout

"My children are grown now and starting families of their own," says Elaine Nelson Thompson. "I began to recognize a generational cycle that I wanted desperately to be broken. My natural mother abandoned me and I had run from my offspring. What was in store for my grandchildren?"[5]

Is it possible to produce healthy, stable adults from troubled and broken families? Are children able to shake off the pangs of rejection and turmoil and complete the growing up process?

Most researchers agree that children are better off when raised by parents whose relationship "is stable, warm, and mutually supportive."[6] But what happens when the roof blows off the family home?

"Everybody has some kind of a stake and a personal hope in the viability of marriage," sociologist Viktor Gecas says, despite statistics that half of all marriages end in divorce.[7]

> A person who grows up in a dysfunctional family tends to be less optimistic about marriage, less trusting of a spouse, and more likely to engage in the kind of negative confrontation that destroys a relationship.[8]

At least three areas of change impact the child almost immediately: finances, family, and feelings.

The Economic Picture

Especially if the mother runs with the kids, income levels drop, often below the poverty line. There's a change in schools, usually with no opportunity to attend the better ones. Job choices can be minimal. Family needs and stress further impede quality job skills.

A typical set of circumstances is set in motion: substandard educational opportunities, problems in school, grade failures, tendency to drop out, less college, fewer occupational choices, lower income.

If only the economic status of the child has been effected, that shapes "certain features of the life course."[9] One gift older generations can give to the younger is hope for the future, a boost toward training for jobs and careers so they will be able to provide for themselves as well as or better than their parents did.

The most effective weapons against poverty and downward economic spiral are marriage and a stable family. But being poor, of course, doesn't guarantee a poor quality of life, just as gaining riches can't promise happiness. However, a desertion by an adult that results in destitution or loss of vital resources stunts the launching of the family's youngest members and invites lifelong resentments.

The Family Structure

With the increasing divorce rate and the breakdown of the extended family, very few young people can turn back to their own families for support. That is very tragic because we're not handing anything on from one generation to another.[10]

Did you hug your child today? the bumper stickers urge.

When an adult runs, contact with children by one of the parents is decreased. The actual number of hours devoted to the kids is drastically reduced, in "attention, help, and supervision."[11] One of the most basic losses to children is the role modeling in learning a basic social skill: how to work through challenges and problems. Families are supposed to teach one another how to live, not how to escape from life.

Families exist for nurturing the young, for "the provision of emotional support, intimacy, and love," and for developing deeply rooted attachments to other human beings.[12]

Many times a child from a broken home will lose contact with other key family members such as grandparents, aunts, uncles, and cousins. With little or no supervision by loving caretakers, kids are vulnerable to negative influences. Parents can quickly get out of touch with their kids. Children keep growing, changing, assessing—and they're very sensitive. Absence speaks to them louder than words do.

Fears can settle in: a woman can't be trusted—when you least expect it, she'll disappear, even if she's your mother, your wife, or your very best friend.

"I was afraid of marriage for a long time. When I finally fell hard for a woman, I expected it wouldn't last. Surely I had some of the same deadly faults that my father had. Whenever we disagreed or argued I told myself, 'This is it. She's gone.' "

"We do not have a family-friendly society," says sociology professor Arlie Hochschild, author of the landmark study about two-career marriages, *The Second Shift*.[13] The family unit is important to health, wholeness, and well-being. Antagonism and rejection by family members is distressing because we spend more time with these people. We usually have more shared interests and activities, they're our own flesh and blood.

They know more about us—our strengths and weaknesses, our loves and fears, our likes and dislikes—than anyone else. They've entered into public and private privileges of commitments and attachments.

Children can't survive alone.

> Communication with others is a matter of life and death for the child. The possibility of being left alone is necessarily the most serious threat to the child's whole existence.[14]

A counselor notes, "The generation of children who will soon be leaders are, in many cases, emotionally bankrupt when it comes to knowledge of the 'traditional family.' I think the survivor instinct has developed as children feel abandoned and ripped off in the loving parent department."[15]

A child of a very nontraditional family comments, "My grandmother abandoned her family when my dad was in his teens. He vowed never to marry. I'm the product of one of his girlfriends. Family disruption is normal for me. I don't even know who my family is."

There are many ways to destroy a family. Running away is one.

The Emotional Merry-Go-Round

After studying 131 children of divorce over a span of fifteen years, Judith Wallerstein, the California clinical psychologist who first raised public awareness of the lasting damage of divorce, found them to be at higher risk for depression, poor grades, substance abuse, and intimacy problems.

"We started to report this," she says, "and people got angry. They said, 'Impossible! If it's good for the parents, it's good for the children.' "[16]

Love is learned, sheltered, and nurtured in an I-care-no-matter-what schoolroom. When class is called on account of lack of love, children become young adults who have no clue how to give it or receive it.

"One day my world felt happy, secure. The next day I was suddenly lost in a forest of terrifying creatures. The terrifying creatures at one time had been my friends, my family. Now, they seemed strange, like ferocious animals ready to strike. I was only four. My mother had run away."

Children can feel angry toward one parent, protective toward another. They can worry the situation is all their fault. They wonder what will happen to them. They want to fix the problem. Then, they're depressed.

They develop problems at school. They may try to create a crisis to divert the attention of the adults in their world. They're burdened with keeping secrets of one parent from another. They feel forced into disloyalty. Sometimes they're not allowed to talk about the past. Anxiety builds.

Emotions range from rage to guilt, from resignation to despair. They hope and pray she'll come back, or that their family will be reunited. They feel betrayed, abandoned, unloved.

Being a child of a mother who runs away leads to a lack of respect and trust of adults. Tenseness builds if quarrels or unsettled dilemmas continue. A kid can feel ignored or in the way. The emotional climate of the adults leaves no room for the feelings of the child.

Sides have to be taken.

Friends shy away because of this bad thing that happened.

Kids tell it in their own words:

"My mom ran away when I was only five. I struggled with the guilt and loneliness and feelings that I was ugly and bad for years. Then, one day I realized that I had faced probably the toughest thing in life I'd ever face, and I survived. Perhaps I had something to offer the world after all. But what you experience as a kid sometimes takes a long while to get over. The question, why you are unwanted, becomes the central theme of your existence."

"I wanted to run away too. But I didn't have any money, or anywhere to go. I wanted to find my mother and beg her to take me with her. Sometimes the agony was so intense I felt I was nearly suffocating. All these desires just made me frustrated and I began to hate her . . . that she could go and I couldn't . . . that she would leave and not include me."

"Because my parents were going through terrible times, they didn't have time for the old me as the 'kid,' so that I had to become an adult much quicker in a sense."[17]

The stages of coping for the abandoned resembles those experiencing other kinds of loss or grief:
(a) Denial: "She's coming back!"
(b) Anger and humiliation: "How could she do this to me?"
(c) Bargaining and desperation: "Everything will be different this time."
(d) Acceptance: "I've got my life to live somehow."
(e) Growth: "I made mistakes. She made mistakes. I'll learn as much as I can. Nothing's wasted."
Reuben says, "I was almost eight when she suddenly disappeared. It was like she died, only she could appear at anytime. I thought of her like a ghost who might come back to haunt me or an angel who would protect me. I suppose I thought it would help me with the pain somehow, to make her seem surreal. But it only prolonged it."

Tracy, now twenty-one years old, offers this advice through her own growth experience: "Forgive yourself for all the mistakes you've made. Especially a child can feel it's all her fault somehow. More important, try to understand why the runaway did what she did. Try to forgive her. Anger and bitterness ruin a life far more than facing a sad situation squarely."

In areas like Atlanta, Georgia, parents who want to split are being ordered back to school to learn how divorce will affect their kids. Six thousand parents have already taken a four-hour course called "Children Cope with Divorce."

"I want people to understand what it is that divorce does to children and what they can avoid . . . how easy it [can be] to forget about children when you're involved in an adversarial situation," said DeKalb County Superior Court Judge Robert J. Castellani.

The class, developed by a Cobb County court official, is offered by the nonprofit social service agency Families First. Among other things they teach parents not to use children as messengers or weapons to get back at a spouse. The goal is to let go, forgive, in order to provide a decent life for a child.[18]

Divided Needs of Adults and Children

We can dwell on all the needs of a woman—why she's tempted to chuck it all, why she's driven to run—but we're hard-pressed to find the benefits for children.

> When parenting competes with other adult interests
> and roles, we increasingly acknowledge the legitimacy
> of self-interest.[19]

Adults in crisis—frequently, the adult comes first, the child last. It's assumed the child will survive, somehow. After all, this doesn't concern him or her. If the child reveals no inner distress, he may be ignored completely. If the child expresses worry or has fits, the adult may resent the lack of support from the child.

> We have entered an era in which individuals are very focused on themselves and their situation, and are increasingly unwilling to focus on the needs of others.[20]

One man was so angry his wife ran off that he called her terrible names whenever the children mentioned her. How could they, immersed in such constant condemnation, dare say or think a nice word about her ever again?

Samantha Mathis, a young actress, was separated from her actress mother, Bibi Besch, for long periods of time. "A mom can't just sacrifice her dreams and her life for her children. That just wouldn't be right. But, as a teenager, it's not so easy to see it from your parents' perspective, and there were certainly times when I was more into my anger and disappointment. . . . When I graduated from grade school—I was thirteen—my mother was in Rome. . . . The other kids had their mothers, and I had my grandmother. It was nice that she could be there, but I wanted my mother. . . . One thing I would do differently, though. Sometimes I sat on my feelings and anger, and I think you have to ask for what you need and not assume your parents always know when you really need them."[21]

"I remember when I was real little, we went with my dad to visit one of his girlfriends, and he said, 'Don't talk about your mom.' Even now, I try not to talk about my mom—things we do. Or, like, if I have a shawl on that Mom bought me, I try not to mention that, because I don't know if my dad wants me to. I don't think you should ever say to a child, 'Don't talk about your mom.' They're part of your life."[22]

A father finally realized, "I was forcing my children to try to forget their mother, to put her out of their minds and hearts, to never discuss her. The damage showed in their attitudes at school, their behavior towards each other, and their acceptance of me as an imperfect father."

The motives and perceptions of adults and the needs of children sometimes clash—with tragic results. In another kind of case, women and children are often the prime targets of domestic violence. This provokes other choices: sheltering and feeding the kids or fleeing the abuse.

Self-Fulfilling Prophecies Unlimited

Close kin of runaways discover new perceptions of themselves by others. "What is so wrong with you that she had to escape like that?" "No wonder you're having such problems [at work, in school, getting along with people, gaining weight, losing weight]. It's to be expected." The stares. The looks of pity. The frowns. The whispers along the sidewalks. Overnight the abandoned ones become the watched ones. It's as if the runaway sprayed glittered Xs on all those she passed on her way to the escape hatch. In the beginning, at least, the runaway finds relief and the hope of starting over; the "left-behinds" bear the brunt of public scrutiny and inquisition.

"One of my teachers wanted to know if there was another man. I really didn't know. But even if I did, I wouldn't want to tell her. I guess she thought because I was a kid she could pry some information without seeming nosy. I sure thought she was nosy."

But the abandoned ones themselves may suddenly see themselves differently. They can indulge in long periods of self-examination and project self-fulfilling prophecies about their human faults or the damage that has been done to them by one who ran. The expectation of harm yields to embracing the harm, rather than over-coming.

Some children as they reach their teens toy with a means of revenge against the runaway adult. The adult is inaccessible, so they take it out on themselves.

> If for any reason other persons cannot become the object of an individual's destructiveness, his own self easily becomes the object. When this happens in a marked degree, physical illness is often the result, and even suicide may be attempted.[23]

The Throwaways

While the runaway is absent through an act of her own volition, the throwaway had no alternative, that is, she was forced to leave home. She was rejected and shoved out by her caretaker or peer. Many of these are the homeless on our city streets.

Alicen explains how it was for her. "I have four children, but I've never felt comfortable in the 'Mom' role. Especially when my kids became teens. They changed so much. I really didn't want them around and they knew it. Each one of them left home by the time they were fifteen. It got so I even encouraged them. I haven't heard from any of them since, except the youngest. I might let her come back . . . just on a trial basis."

Standing in the Gap

> Do your best to come to me quickly, for Demas, because he loved this world, has deserted me.
>
> 2 Timothy 4:9–10

When a woman runs she leaves a gap, a hole, a wrenching absence. Someone may need to fill it. At least for a time.

How do we attempt to make a heavenly blessing out of an earthly wreck?

By ministering peace in the crush of turmoil. By working through the transition awkwardness, by nursing the fragile bonds that remain, by becoming one of those select persons who are able to "forge continuity out of chaos."[24]

When someone runs, someone else is left to pick up the pieces and mop up the mess. Emergency aid is required to minimize the damage.

Reaching out to the spurned, forsaken, and discarded requires special understanding—giving assurances that we'll be there for them, that their feelings are important, that we'll check on them frequently. This is especially important for children, who, through no fault of their own "have lost their security and find their hearts confused and torn."[25]

People who stand in the gap can't meet every need. We do the things we can. We try to adapt when some action's not working. We try not to be dragged to the depths of despair.

Filling the gap is not the final solution. It's interim work. We're temporary help. Rebuilding by the injured parties brings closure to a gaping episode.

The ones who stand in the gap have extra (and unfair) burdens to bear—many times the abandoned, in their need to vent their hostilities, will explode to those targets nearest and most available to them. They really want to hurt the one who hurt them. But that one is gone.

However, in the mire of the unpleasantness lessons can be gleaned.

> Learning how best to cope with abandonment—and with the reunion that often follows abandonment—may give us insights into better ways of coping with other traumatic and disturbing family experiences. We are them and they are us.[26]

When Troubles Come In Bunches

"I was overwhelmed. Not only did my best friend run away, but my neighbor found out she had cancer, my husband lost the best secretary he'd ever had, and I had just agreed to serve on the Pastor Seeking Committee after a tense resignation. Serious, urgent needs . . . how could I possibly meet them all?"

"You picked a fine time to leave me, Lucille," Kenny Rogers sings. Adults who run don't always choose the most convenient moment for the sake of all concerned. In fact, if the whole truth were known, penetrating spiritual warfare is heavy at such a time as this. Many are in the valley of decision. Trials and testings and tribulations abound. One ran, but countless others were greatly troubled.

In this environment, reaching out to the wounded becomes a hit-and-miss affair, not the carefully crafted steps of the alert, practiced, ready, and fully available attendant.

We need to determine how much we can give.

In the meantime, we call on heaven and trust God to fill in *our* gaps.

Discovery Questions

1. Read Nehemiah 4:7–15.
   Describe what is happening.
   How did they effectively frustrate the enemy?
   Has anyone ever had to "stand in the gap" for you?
   Explain.

2. What would be your motivation for reaching out to help an abandoned child? An adult?
   What would you most want to do?
   What would you be careful *not* to do?

3. What do you think would be the greatest repercussion for a person who was rejected by someone he or she loved?

What would be an effective way to overcome the pain and injury?

4. Read the following quote from *Time* magazine:

> America treats its children like excess baggage. In all other countries, childbirth is seen as an event that is vitally important to the life and future of the nation. But in the U.S. we treat child rearing as some kind of expensive private hobby.[27]

Why do you think this is true? Or do you?

5. Tony is eight, dark-haired, brown-eyed, and his mother ran away six months ago. Jessica is eight, dark-haired, brown-eyed, and her mother is devoted to and content with her family.

What do you think about Tony?

What do you think about Jessica?

If it isn't the same, why not?

Which one would you rather your own children played with and why?

6. The former husband (the custodial parent) of a run-away wife complains: "Between my job hassles and crisis parenting and trying to keep up with the house, I hardly know who I am anymore. I've lost my identity." How would you respond to this man?

Notes

[1] *The Day America Told the Truth*, reported in "What Are You Willing to Do for $10 Million?" *Discipleship Journal* (September/October 1991): 16.

[2] Bogle, letter.

[3] Bonnie G. Wheeler, "Just As I Am," *Sunday Digest*, 23 February 1986, 5.

[4] Frank F. Furstenburg, Jr., "Divorce and the American Family," *Annual Review of Sociology* (1990): 384.

[5] E. N. Thompson, interview.

[6] Furstenburg, "Divorce and the American Family," 390.

[7] Jim Jacobs, "Charmed Relationships," *Lewiston* (Idaho) *Morning Tribune*, 12 February 1995, A 1.

[8] Ibid., A 5.

[9] Furstenburg, "Divorce and the American Family," 390.

[10] T. Berry Brazelton, M.D., interview by Bill Moyers, *A World of Ideas*, ed. Betty Sue Flowers (New York: Doubleday, 1989), 140.

[11] Paul R. Amato and Bruce Keith, "Parental Divorce and Adult Well-Being: A Meta-analysis," *Journal of Marriage and the Family* (February 1991): 44.

[12] Gove, Style, and Hughes, "Effect of Marriage," 22–23.

[13] Elizabeth Gleick, "Should This Marriage Be Saved?" *Time*, 27 February 1995, 53.

[14] Fromm, *Escape from Freedom*, 21.

[15] Bogle, letter.

[16] Gleick, "Should This Marriage Be Saved?" 52.

[17] Eric E. Rofes, ed., *The Kids' Book of Divorce* (New York: Vintage Books, 1982), 114.

[18] Associated Press, "Parents on Edge of Divorce Go to Class," *Lewiston* (Idaho) *Morning Tribune*, 17 October 1991, A2.

[19] Graham B. Spanier, "Bequeathing Family Continuity," *Journal of Marriage and the Family* (February 1989): 5.

[20] Gove, Style, and Hughes, "Effect of Marriage," 27.

[21] Lynn Minton, "Fresh Voices," *Parade*, 23 February 1992, 14.

[22] Minton, "What Children of Divorce Want Parents to Know," *Parade*, 2 March 1992, 14.

[23] Fromm, *Escape from Freedom*, 180.

[24] Spanier, "Bequeathing Family Continuity," 11.

[25] Stowell, "The Divorce Dilemma," *Moody*, November 1991, 15.

[26] Brenton, *The Runaways*, 17.

[27] Sylvia Ann Hewlett, "Watching a Generation Waste Away," interview by Janice Castro, *Time*, 26 August 1991, 10.

Seven

Of Cold Winter Fogs and Traffic Jams
Dealing with Regret

Is a runaway ever sorry? Does she ever cast a longing, lingering look behind her? Does running produce an aching void or a weight on her mind? Or is it pure R-E-L-I-E-F?

September 1993 newspapers headlined Katherine Power, 44, one of the F.B.I.'s most-wanted fugitives, emerging from twenty-three years of hiding. She surrendered to authorities for charges in an armed bank robbery at a National Guard armory in which a policeman was slain. She drove the getaway car.

Katherine Power—banker's daughter, valedictorian, winner of a Betty Crocker homemaker award, anti-war radical—ran after the robbery with Susan Saxe, a fellow student from Brandeis University. They evaded capture by hiding out in women's communes.

Susan was arrested in Philadelphia in 1975. Katherine assumed an alias as a cook and restaurant owner in a small Oregon town. Her fourteen-year-old son and her husband were thunderstruck to learn her true identity.[1]

Asked why she had surrendered after all that time, she stated that she finally deliberated on how "someone

105

such as myself could commit such outrageously illegal acts." She decided to take responsibility.

"This building isn't big enough to contain my grief," her husband responded at his wife's arraignment.

"I am deeply sorry for the damage my actions have caused both particular individuals and society. I will continue to live my life as an act of contrition for that damage," she told the judge.[2]

Katherine faced a long and bittersweet road home: reunion with her relatives, facing the dead policeman's family, a minimum five years in federal prison and a $10,000 fine.

Some who run live with regret.

Some who run return to face the consequences as they seek to make amends.

Some who run are surprised to realize that they look back on their former life in positive terms, and find similar negative behavior repeated in the present.

An adult runaway performs a public vanishing act. She steals away from kith and kin and connections. She burrows herself in a private hideaway for reasons uniquely her own. She fades from one scene and materializes in another. But the way is not always smooth. Difficulties emerge. Frustrations abound. Inner wars complicate the process.

The runaway often finds that "[she] has to rely on old habits in order to cope with confusing new surroundings." Some flee from families and friends only to find themselves "attempting to escape further by running away from themselves."[3]

Some run and wallow in a mire of remorse.

The State of Being Sorry

Sometimes the runaway succeeds in [her] bold venture. More often [she] does not. [She] can become dispirited to find that geographic change does little or nothing to eradicate old fears, firmly established habits, and an inability to cope.[4]

"I was always on the go, frantically speeding from one project to another, one meeting to another. I couldn't stand to be alone, not for a moment. Then one day the lady in the apartment down the hall innocently asked me, 'What are you running from?' Her comment touched a deep nerve. I knew it was time to sit still and work through some feelings . . . and, yes, some regrets."

"This is a very hard time for me because I'm realizing how much my actions hurt the ones I love."

Captain Frank Patchett, head of the Missing Persons Bureau of the Los Angeles Police Department, affirms: "Nearly every man or woman who deserts his or her spouse regrets having done so; the majority lament that they would give anything to be back living their former lives. But many of them figure they have cut their bridges."[5]

Regret is expressed in countless ways.

Regret can be grief over what she lost, or disappointment in what she hoped to gain.

Regret can be momentary, random, and occasional. Or regret can be constant and chronic, a deep melancholy or depression.

Regret can be excruciating to face, impossible to console, or it can be a mood that's quickly shaken off.

We can regret the hurt we've caused others, or the harm we've done to ourselves.

A friend told me about Carlene. She's certainly not the classic runaway. In fact, the day she left town they threw a big going-away party for her.

Carlene ventured into the world to seek her fortune, to master her fate, to plumb the heights of career and freedom. Now, twenty years later, I'm visiting her in the psychiatric ward of a state hospital. Carlene shared with me parts of her story.

"I have an earned doctorate. I've traveled the globe and held jobs on several continents. I've been engaged three times to two different men. Twice I called it off; the last time he did. I'm forty-two years old and have no husband, no children. My parents are gone. My siblings and friends don't know me anymore and don't know what to do with me. I can't hold a job . . . I take heavy doses of antidepressants and tranquilizers. One drink and I'm over the edge . . . and on the outside I can't seem to stay away from the stuff.

"It's a nightmare. I can't believe I'm stuck in here. I don't get no respect. They've got me labeled. I'm in quarantine for suicide watch. I feel like such a failure. What did I do that was so wrong? Why am I here? I took a bad turn somewhere and there seems to be no way out . . . I don't think of myself as a runaway. Not really. I just somehow drifted and disconnected."

Drifted and Disconnected

Running away doesn't have to be sudden; we can gradually slip, slide away. A decision here, a choice there that separates and sweeps us far away from our center that we call home. One day we realize we're among the missing, we're awash on some alien shore. We're alone, with only our regrets.

We can regret either our actions, or the consequences of our deeds.

We may grieve silently, privately, or bemoan loudly the pathetic falling of our lot.

Regret can stir twinges of conscience or prolonged sieges of suffering.

There may be sorrow without repentance, when we're sorry for the consequences only, but never true repentance without sorrow.

The word for *repentance* in Greek means to turn round or have a change of heart and attitude. Repentance involves being sincerely sorry for our sin and willing to change direction.[6]

Sometimes running produces only slight misfortunes. For others it's death to all the runaway once knew and would like to reclaim. Perhaps she intended her running to be temporary, but the door slammed tight behind her.

The Many Shades of Remorse

You have taken from me my closest friends
and have made me repulsive to them.
I am confined and cannot escape;
my eyes are dim with grief. . . .
the darkness is my closest friend.

Psalm 88:8–9a,18

We all go through times of change in identity and circumstance that are out of our control—when we experience any loss: the death of a loved one, job layoff or being fired from a job, a major reverse in finances, a forced move, breakdown in health, aging, being torn away from nurturing friends.

As we work through the grieving and adjustment period, the moment comes when we know we must move on. To cling to the old identity is unreality, a stunting of growth, childish. It's a kind of running away.

But when change occurs by our deliberate action and erupts like a bomb, we'd like a chance to do that one over again.

If we run out of anger, bitterness, or revenge we may never heal or grow beyond what we were the day we ran. Our inner life freezes until we deal with the regret of the lost years and release them.

The Two Sides of Shame

Shame has to do with the sense of right and wrong. Shame falls somewhere between mild embarrassment and cruel humiliation. The goal is not mere retribution but conformity—good conformity, the kind that makes it easier for people to form communities.[7]

Feeling shame can result from a negative slur or a redemptive prod. The one shamed can lose face or determine to be vindicated. Rather than an ostracizing punishment some will see "feeling shame as a way back to the fold."[8]

Mortification. Stigma. Humility. A sense of morality and mutual responsibility. Deep penitence and eagerness to make things right. Some of these traits and conditions prepare the way for true repentance, a growing private and profound sense of regret. But shame can also be a public humiliation. Two different paths and usually two separate results.

Shame is also "a soul-deep sense that *there is something uniquely wrong with me* that is not wrong with you or anyone else in the world. . . . It isn't just that I *make* a mistake . . . I *am* a mistake."[9]

The burden of guilt and regret can make freedom an unbearable burden. To find relief the runaway may leave one confinement only to enter another, still feeling insignificant and powerless. She may indulge in guilt trips or lambaste herself or someone nearby every time she remembers an incident from the past. Or she may brood, seeing herself as a victim or the heroine of a great tragedy.

"I was a rotten mother, I know, and I didn't want to be around them [the children]," recalls Jane, an alcoholic who went on periodic binges and learned to stay sober only after she had left home. "I knew their father would take good care of them. But this motherhood thing is so strong. When you're still a little girl they begin stuffing you with it. Even though I knew I was doing everyone a favor, I still felt like I'd committed the crime of the century. It was so illogical. I was a lousy mother but I kept thinking how I'd let them down by leaving—when the fact is, I let them down every day I was with them."[10]

A runaway woman's deepest regret often concerns her children—"the feeling of having hurt them and often not being able to participate in their adult lives."[11]

Another runaway mother described these attacks of guilt as "just like time bombs—thought I'd explode."[12]

Elaine Nelson Thompson states that, "I was most sorry that I felt so beaten down and of 'no worth' that I did not fight to keep my children. . . . I felt at the time and even now that it was the right choice economically. I did not have the means to support my children as they were used to. All I had were my own clothes and an old junker car. My husband could provide for their every physical need. . . . My regret is that in making that decision it came across to my children that I didn't care, which couldn't have been further from the truth. I really struggled with the guilt . . . the way I left and the damage it was doing to my children. I had now entered the world of the outcast, the leper, and my kids felt unclean in touching me.

"I'm not sure I could have done things differently, given my emotional and physical state at the time. But looking back, from this vantage point, I would have given much more effort to ensure that my children knew how much I loved them. I also would have been more honest with them about how hurt I was. I don't think I was really aware of all that was going on with me then."

Remorse may show itself through a variety of symptoms:

- depression
- irritability

- constant frustration
- chronic sickness
- obsessive busyness
- hopelessness
- difficulty making decisions
- desperation

One counselor explains: "I think regret is there, but often so buried that it takes a long time to identify. There is at first the strong desire to find themselves and live to meet their needs."[13]

These women express how it has been for them:

"Running away has affected every part of my life. Because I ran to make something of myself, I've become obsessed with that. Everything I do has got to be bigger, better than anyone else. This compulsion has made me a nervous wreck. I can't just enjoy life."

"If I could have known ahead of time the consequences of my running away, I would have stayed. I would have figured some way of working out what at the time seemed so unbearable."

"For several years after I ran I loudly and vehemently encouraged other women I knew to run too. I was trying so hard to prove what I did was right. When I finally began to feel the regret and deep sorrow for what I did, there was nowhere for me to turn because I was supposed to be so together, so okay after I had the courage to do what I did."

"I ran away because I wanted to pursue ambitions that I felt had been denied me. For several years I immersed myself in the career game. Then, one day it hit me. I was dying inside because of the indifference. People in my company used one another like the products we designed. Everyone was in pursuit of their own interests. We were objects to be manipulated for promotion plums or customer approval. The fulfillment I longed for was stifled in the recognition wars, the bonus haggling and the nit-picking over work sheets and over-time."

"For many years I blamed others for my running away—the pressures I was put under, the difficult situations I faced, the lack of love I felt—but real freedom came to me when I finally realized I ran because of my own convenience, my own selfishness, my reluctance to vigorously seek solutions. When I shouldered the burden squarely on myself, I finally stopped running. I took a stand for truth from where I was right then."

"I stopped going to church, which was a big mistake. I blamed God for not changing my situation so I wouldn't need to run. If I had continued to go to church and stayed faithful in prayer and Bible study, I know I would have understood things sooner, would have received better help."

"I always feel as though a perpetual apology is expected. When people get to know me, and then find out what I've done, they're torn in their convictions . . . of what they think of women runaways, and then how they feel about me."

"My relationship with my family deteriorated to the point that I thought I was willing to pay the cost of running away. But that, of course, increased our mutual bitterness. The emotional consequences are so complex and painful. I expect only hostility if I try to reconcile. But lately I've been thinking about my elderly grandmother . . . I could almost do it for love of her, to make a semblance of peace before she dies."

Some runaways desire a fresh beginning. They feel doomed by failure, dragged down by guilt. They need a way out—out of the past to forge a new now.

One choice leads to another, and then to another. Now their lives are strewn with the memorials and wreckage. But they can't ever go back, not entirely.

But can they work to make a different ending?

Discovery Questions

1. What has been your biggest regret?
   What can you do about it now?

2. What are you committed to, no matter what? Why?

3. Read Luke 22:31–34. What does this tell us about spiritual warfare? What does this reveal about human nature? How could a runaway redeem herself?

4. Share an experience when a church, church leader, or lay counselor took positive, biblical steps and restored an estranged, hurting person to full fellowship.
   What were the steps that brought about this resolution?

Notes

[1] John Curran, "An End to Her Fugitive Life," *Lewiston* (Idaho) *Morning Tribune*, 16 September 1993, A 1,9.

[2] Martin Finucane, "Katherine Ann Power Gets Five Years," *Lewiston* (Idaho) *Morning Tribune*, 25 November 1993, C10.

[3] Rowell, "Adult Runaways," 69.

[4] Ibid.

[5] Ibid.

[6] Robin Keeley, ed., *Eerdmans' Handbook to Christian Belief* (Grand Rapids: Eerdmans, 1982), 336.

[7] Jonathan Alter and Pat Wingert, "The Return of Shame," *Newsweek*, 6 February 1995, 22.

[8] Ibid., 23.

[9] Sandra Wilson, review of Shame-Free Parenting, *Christian Journal of Psychology and Counseling* 7, no. 3 (July 1992): 20.

[10] Brenton, *The Runaways*, 136.

[11] Alexandre, in letter to author, 28 January 1992.

[12] Brenton, *The Runaways*, 136.

[13] Bogle, in letter to author, 26 January 1992.

Eight

The Long Road Home
The Fragile Steps to Reconciliation

> Show me, O LORD, my life's end
> and the number of my days;
> let me know how fleeting is my life.
> Psalm 39:4

Mary is thirty-two years old. At age sixteen she moved out on her own. At twenty-two she moved twelve hundred miles from home and didn't communicate with her mother for ten years. Last year Mary made some calls and wrote some letters to reestablish this relationship. A few months ago Mary's mother discovered she had lung cancer. In a matter of weeks she died.

"It's not fair!" Mary wails. "I was just beginning to realize I had a mother. Now she's gone!"

Alas . . . the fleeting years slip by.[1]

How fragile is this sinew of generations.[2]

Runaways who are "seeking some nameless new freedom can easily become outcasts who wistfully yearn for the comforting fetters of their former lives."[3]

117

Minimizing the Damage

Qualms about the future, doubts about the present, misgivings about the past—these unsettling thoughts can replace the former confidence or desperation the runaway once knew. So can a change in beliefs or standards, or finding a new ethic or principle of life to embrace.

Integrity. Character. Decency. Honesty. Honor. Trust. Loyalty. Each of these words rings with richness. An enlightened woman will seek to smooth out the haste and fallout and rudeness of a former run. Apologies and much more are in order.

Theologian and ethicist Richard Mouw explains the dilemma for all who have freedom of choice: "What may start as a simple decision can be difficult to undo. It may take a lot of work. It may take people helping us in complicated and professional ways to undo the power of sin in our lives."[4]

Those who want to make restitution may need help along the way. Repentant runaways may need mediators between them and the hurts of the abandoned.

"Blessed are the peacemakers," encourages Matthew 5:9. Barnabas paved the way of peace for Paul, the converted enemy. Later, Paul interceded for Onesimus, not only a runaway slave, but also a thief. (See Philemon and Acts 9:26–28.)

> When the flood waters of the cesspool have come up to your very soul, you don't need challenges; you need COMFORT. You need a friend to come alongside and say, "I am hurting with you . . . I am standing with you . . . I am weeping with you. I am undergirding you as best I can. Link your shield of faith with mine and somehow we will make it together."[5]

Repentance for the potential runaway is so much easier. When apprehensions and forebodings cause her to hesitate, the main changes she must make are mostly in her mind, her vision of her present world, the way she thinks. She still has time to work it through. She can practice self-control and restraint, refraining from impulses and drives. She can also vigorously seek alternative solutions. Once she actually runs back-tracking means endless explanations and repairs and promises to counteract the betrayals. Much time and effort and patience will be required to reestablish trust.

Restitution is "a long process . . . and it begins with support."[6]

Some Ways To Really Say "I'm Sorry"

Where do we begin? How do we begin to resolve the issues of atonement and admission of faults? What do we do beyond saying, "I'm sorry"?

• Accept the present situation, no matter what, just as it is. What can I do from here? What is impossible? With whom from the past can I make contact?

• Determine who I am now. In what ways am I the same, in what ways different, than when I ran away?

• Focus on loss, on grief. What do I truly regret more than anything? With whom do I need to share these thoughts?

• Identify the reason(s) for leaving that way. Why the secrecy? The abruptness?

• Analyze the way I feel now. Am I confused? Determined? Lonely? Pressured? Process the feelings. Discern the main motivation for any plan of action, any interest in reaching out. Experience and express the depths of the emotions at play, then make decisions.

• Perform one specific, practical act toward restitution. Sift all the suggestions and advice you receive. Knowing your situation as you do, what will work best? Try to make choices that will foster healing. Create something personal and loving and give it to someone who was hurt: a poem, a letter, a song, a quilt, a cherry cheesecake, a scrapbook. Acknowledge the pain, the loss, the anger of the one abandoned. Purpose to recognize this person's need, not to rationalize the choice. Assure this person that he or she is loved, that there's been a change of heart.

• Ask forgiveness. However, focus on forgiving self and accepting God's forgiveness. Expect negative repercussions from some quarter—lingering feelings of resentment, unfair demands that take advantage of your guilt feelings, tense communications, blame for behavior problems of affected parties, lack of trust or respect.

• Watch and wait as the process of restitution unfolds quietly, steadily, slowly—and with surprises.

• Don't expect those with whom you reconcile to fill all the voids in your life.

• At the right time, if appropriate, present a list of grievances along with a reporting of what you intend to do differently. Deep repentance involves "both sorrow for sin and a determination to change."[7]

Runaway women share their struggles in trying to wave a white flag of truce and peace:

"I first had to deal with my own feelings of bitterness and my low self-image. I had grown cold toward my children over the years as a defense mechanism. If I threw up a shield of apathy and unconcern, they couldn't hurt me. This protected my emotions, but it also hardened me. These seasons of coldness grew into estrangement. When I finally determined I wanted to open myself up to my grown children, I had to fight my own habitual responses."

"In order to explain all the context of why I ran, I'd be forced to tell damaging information about key people left behind. There were so many things wrong—what was going on at the time, what had been done in the past—my lashing out couldn't begin to correct things. Besides, I wasn't willing to do that . . . for my children's sake. So, I reaped the condemnation. Years later my kids finally understood so much on their own. It was hard to keep quiet. I paid a great price in the loss of friends. Only a precious few kept reaching out to me without knowing the whole story."

"The hardest thing I ever did in my life was to walk down the aisle at my daughter's wedding. All those eyes watching me, judging me, knowing that I was the mother who ran. If it wasn't for my friends back home, praying for me, caring for me, I never could have done it."

"Making peace was complicated by the fact that I had taken our savings account and some family heirlooms to pawn. That fact more than anything else kept me from trying to return. How could I ever pay this back?"

Whether actually trying to go back, or attempting to communicate and reach out from where she settled, a season is required for healing, for improving, for recuperating from the wounds inflicted. There's an awkwardness stage that must be endured—the pressure of being watched, every word weighed, the self-conscious attempts at politeness. If she returns, she will have to attend to chores long neglected, try to implement changes that may not come off as expected, realize that some things will never change, and feel obliged to offer apology and make amends.

Reunions—Coming Together Again

"Will they want me?"

"What will people say if I go back?"

"How much have they changed? Have I changed?"

Reunions, after a long absence, are disturbing. But reunions "help us connect past, present, and future in a world that often seems all too fragmented and disjointed."[8]

Reunions force us together—to communicate, to reveal our feelings, to work through those blundering transitions, to perhaps reverse our former mindset.

Truth and Consequences

Runaways are a classic example of the truth that while forgiveness through Christ covers sin, "we are yet left living with the fruits of what we have sown . . . the sufficiency of the atonement and the immutability of God's law of sowing and reaping coexist."[9]

> The only way sin can be undone in our lives is by our turning away from our sin and turning to God. There is the hour of decision.[10]

In the lost art of apology, we have neglected the wholly converting act of getting down on our knees. Body posture helps our mind, emotions, and will to get entirely and actively involved. Washing of feet, serving tables, bowing in respect—whatever produces the desired effect for the penitent. We live in a society of shamelessness. We want to feel good about ourselves, no matter what we've done. We don't have a system of absolution because we don't recognize sin. We have to go to the Bible to find the way of change and starting over.

> Says theologian Richard John Neuhaus: We *should* dislike much about ourselves, because there is much about ourselves that is not only profoundly dislikable but odious. It's not for nothing that the Ten Commandments are put in the negative.[11]

Prodigal Daughters

The ideal is that the runaway comes to the end of herself and wants to come "home."

The ideal is that someone stands at the other end waiting for her—anxious for sight of her, arms outstretched, ready to forgive and begin again, gifts in hand, party planned.

The ideal is unconditional love, like the prophet Hosea showed to unfaithful Gomer.

The ideal is happy endings like David Wilkerson tells about. "A young mother of eight children, all born out of wedlock, was restored to the children, whom she had abandoned, and the man who fathered them. Last week I had the privilege of marrying them."[12]

Relationships can be staid as mud, or blessed breezes, or volcanoes waiting to blow. Any of these kinds of bonds, once severed, are not easily repaired. The realities have to do with women who've traveled down the long road home and found everyone out to lunch—women such as Elaine Nelson Thompson.

"One weekend, after a wonderful visit with my children, my heart seemed to be torn out of my body as I drove them back to their home. I realized I had made a terrible mistake in leaving them, or at least, not fighting for them. *Maybe we can make this marriage work*, I thought. How excited I was as I thought about the possibility. I called my husband and asked to talk with him at a restaurant halfway between his place and mine. I remember feeling very tender towards him. I cried all the way there, asking the Lord to make his attitude toward me loving and compassionate, something I had never felt from him before.

"It was worse than ever. As I expressed my desire to work towards reconciliation, the only thing he told me was, 'Tell it to the whole church. Tell them what you did and beg their forgiveness first, then *maybe* there might be a chance.' I had the sinking feeling that this church that had railed against and accused me before would do the same again. I could not do this. I desperately looked for some ounce of love or concern for me as a person. Neither my husband nor his solution provided this need.

"A year later, I again approached my husband. This time he brought an elder from the church to meet with us. The elder did all the talking, mostly quoted scriptures of condemnation. His attitude fed my view that everyone from the church was critical, that no one sensed the scope of my staggering problems or confused perceptions. No one seemed to grasp my desperate need for healing, hope, and compassion. No one asked to hear my side of the tragedy. How could I possibly survive going right back into that same situation, with the added burden of unrelenting shame and the humiliating conditions attached to my uncertain pardon?"

Regrets. A desire to reconcile. Judgment without mercy. Law without love. Worn out from the wars. Where does a prodigal daughter go when she's no longer welcomed home?

A left-behind husband tells of his emotional holocaust: "I didn't want to live with someone I'd made so unhappy. Much later she hinted that she might come back someday. I said no. Something snapped when she ran. I remembered the long silences when I'd ask her what's wrong. I was tired of dealing with it . . . with her."

Even when a runaway seeks to return and is initially welcomed back, she and the abandoned ones will probably exist on emotionally different timetables. The runaway wants to put everything behind her and move on. The left-behinds may still be smarting and hesitant to resume former intimacies until much time has passed—that is, until the runaway's intentions have been tested and more explanations come to light. Meanwhile, some semblance of the initial cause of her run still exists. She will have to deal with the accumulation of long-standing and unresolved differences, frustrations, and resentments.

No Regrets

Some runaways do get away with it.

For some, to have regrets is like Lot's wife turning back to see what happened to Sodom.

"What's done is done," she says. "I'm going on with life."

"I'm happier now than I've ever been," says another. "I don't regret anything except that I didn't run from there sooner. No more drudge and have to's. All I wanted was *myself* back again."

Others chime in with their own themes:

"Everyone tells me how much I lost—the income, my nice apartment, the wardrobe—but when you're really miserable, you don't miss material things."

"I have such peace now; I'm doing such nice things for myself. I like having the freedom to pursue my own interests."

"Running away was the first decision I ever made without the approval of others. I can do what I want, when I want. I have no regrets."

Some runaways are not sorry. Some are content. But that doesn't mean the ones left behind feel the same.

One abandoned daughter had this to say about her unrepentant runaway mother:

"My mother deserted our father and us five kids forty years ago. My father never remarried and never recovered. Because of that situation I've stayed married to the same man for thirty years and tried to be Super Mom to my own kids.

"A year ago I made contact with my mother. We're not healed. We're what you'd call a work in progress. Making peace is hard to do. Most times Mom seems disinterested. But one day she cried so hard I thought she was going to die. Maybe she really does care."

A runaway may never want to go back, but she wants to be sure she's done the right thing—by the response of those left behind, by fully assessing and enjoying her feelings of freedom and gladness "to be out of there!" At some point curiosity arises to know what's going on in the situation she left or she faces "a great deal of ambivalence" about completely cutting ties with the past.

> The first days away from home are often spent deciding if the choice was worth making, as highlighted by this statement: like almost anything else, people don't always know what's out here. You have to be out to see how it feels. Then you can make choices.[13]

Even those with no regrets about the run often face contradictions. New enemies of a different nature sooner or later come to call—isolation, doubts, mistrust, anxieties, lack of security and a feeling of belonging, hostility and defensiveness, resentments, compulsive behavior, a furtive selfishness.

> The selfish person is always anxiously concerned with himself, he is never satisfied, is always restless, always driven by the fear of not getting enough, of missing something, of being deprived of something.[14]

This runaway describes the incongruities: "It was fantastic being away from my situation. I never went back again. But leaving and becoming so outwardly in control of my life didn't solve my problems. Memories from the past would come back in a confusing way at the most unwelcome moments. I needed someone to talk to, but I wasn't close enough to anyone who I thought would understand. I tried to ignore these episodes. Then, I couldn't sleep nights and sometimes I'd get cold sweats in the daytime. But in time I got used to these things. Perhaps if I'd gone to a counselor they could help me figure out what was happening."

A lack of regret can indicate revenge.

Darlene Bogle reports, "One woman told me she didn't feel bad abandoning her child because her father abandoned her. Now at least one man would have to raise a child alone."

A lack of regret can mean the runaway truly found greener pastures.

> Mothers who seem to fare best overall as runaways are those who take their kids along but who were fully in charge of their households even before they left—competent women forced to hold their families together both economically and emotionally.[15]

But even those who run with few or no regrets don't always find what they're looking for, like the bewildered woman who ponders, "All my life I've wanted to be somebody. Now, who was it I wanted to be?"

Some never want to go back.

Others can't return, even if they want to.

Some never escape the uncertainties and confused emotions that persuaded them to run in the first place.

Meanwhile, what is the role of the peacemakers? We face the eternal human predicament—it's so much easier to judge someone else than it is to judge ourselves.

> Compassion doesn't mean accepting whatever people do. And judgment doesn't mean being hard-hearted.[16]

Bonnie Wheeler is trying to make peace. Her mother was a runaway. She is a daughter who regrets the missing relationship with a mother she barely knew. "I wrote to my mother, apologizing for my wrong attitudes, asking her forgiveness, and sharing my love for Jesus. I started dropping her monthly notes, expecting no answers. But about once every three years, Mother does answer, and I keep writing."[17]

Discovery Questions

1. We've discussed much thus far about the harm a broken family brings to children. Yet, Graham B. Spanier of Oregon State University wonders: "Why do many children, like me, experience abuse, disruption, poverty, or hunger, yet somehow, against great odds, reach adulthood with the notion that family life can be rewarding? . . . In nearly two decades of teaching I have read hundreds of term papers reflecting a powerful commitment to marriage and family written by students who were born into families that could aptly be described as unhappy, broken, pathological, or even nonexistent."[18]

How do you respond to these comments?

In your observation, what effect has the turmoil in family life had on the people around you?

2. Read John 10:10 and Job 2:4–7.
What purpose, if any, does evil have in this world?

What can we do to overcome or counteract it?

3. Which story or statement in this chapter troubled you most? Why?

4. Tell of a time when you struggled between showing mercy or doing justice. Or a time when you had to choose between duty or love?

Have you ever faced a situation where you were divided in your loyalties? How did you handle it? Was this a satisfying solution for all concerned?

5. What do you think are some of the (a) hazards and (b) rewards of feeling and expressing compassion to wrongdoers?

Notes

[1]Horace, *Epodes* 14.1.1.

[2]Ellen Goodman, "When an Aging Aunt Hands You the Bird," *Lewiston* (Idaho) *Morning Tribune*, 23 November 1989, F1.

[3]Rowell, "Adult Runaways," 70.

[4]Richard Mouw, "The Life of Bondage in the Light of Grace," interviewed by David Neff, *Christianity Today*, 9 December 1988, 41.

[5]Barbara Johnson, *Pack Up Your Gloomees in a Great Big Box* (Dallas: Word, 1993), 13.

[6]Bogle, letter.

[7]Keeley, *Eerdmans' Handbook to Christian Belief*, 371.

[8]Timothy Solberg, "Our Faith Reminds Us of Daily Reunions," *Lewiston* (Idaho) *Morning Tribune*, 19 October 1991, B6.

[9]J. Thompson and P. Thompson, *Dance of the Broken Heart*, 97.

[10]Mouw, interview, 41.

[11]Alter and Wingert, "The Return of Shame," 22.

[12]David Wilkerson, *World Challenge Inc. Newsletter*, August 1993.

[13]Palenski and Launer, "Running Away," 356–7.

[14]Fromm, *Escape from Freedom*, 116.

[15]Brenton, *The Runaways*, 136.

[16]Alter and Wingert, "The Return of Shame," 24.

[17]Wheeler, "Just As I Am," 7.

[18]Spanier, "Bequeathing Family Continuity," 4.

Nine

Rainbows Over Angry Skies
Curbing the Urge to Run:
Part One

I did make a good beginning.
Seneca

Oh! If only I knew I would hold out to the last.
Thomas á Kempis

At thirty-three Phyllis is a single parent of two.

She and the kids are crammed into a clapboard rental instead of the sprawling adobe Spanish style home she used to share with her husband, Drew. He's still living there, with Susan.

Phyllis works for a large insurance company—long, stressful hours that leave little time and energy for her children during the week. Most weekends they spend with Drew and Susan.

Recently a miscalculation caused a customer to lose out on a claim. The mistake haunts her. Will she be fired? Will the customer sue? How can she bear to face either? She'd rather not be working in the first place. Perhaps she should quit. But what about her bills?

One weekend she readied Darci and David for the trip to their dad's. She discovered a rose colored dress she'd never seen before crammed in her daughter's suitcase.

"It's for Daddy's wedding," Darci explained. Then, she noticed the look on her mother's face. "Oh, didn't you know?"

Phyllis dreaded the painful drive down the once familiar streets and the few moments of enduring Drew's apathetic eyes, the eyes that once lit with fire at sight of her.

On the way home Phyllis idled at the road on a hill that led south back to the dark, dank apartment—or north, straight out of town. It was the first moment of thrill and anticipation she'd felt in nearly two years. With one firm step to the gas she could leave all the heartache behind.

They can have each other. Let them hurt for once. Let them squirm and suffer. Susan can hassle raising two active stepkids. Drew can pay their full support. And I will be free.

What will be the outcome for Phyllis if she goes? If she stays? What resources can she call upon for the long haul of sticking it out, being faithful, while she's living the consequence of someone close who ran from her?

Faithfulness.

Women like you and me—women like Phyllis—aspire to this high goal. But at moments we're tempted to run. Reaping what we sow often takes place years, even decades, down the road. What can keep us going in gutsy plodding when breaking the fence looks so good? What will help to pull us out of the ruts when a situation's murky, when an important relationship's strained?

What can a woman do to curb the urge to run away? Which of these would we choose?

- Trust her heart; follow her feelings.
- Listen to the opinions of others.

- Sink into depression.
- Resign herself to her situation.
- Deny there are any problems.
- Be guided by a standard outside herself.
- Find help.
- Get away.
- Other:

We're all different. We're each a mix of personality types, contradictions, and complexities in the ways we relate to people and circumstances. We want different things. We differ in motives, beliefs, drives. We also are distinct in how we best handle internal and external pressure. There are almost as many escape routes and stress relievers as there are people.

When a Woman Needs a Break

Sometimes it seems that every moment belongs to someone else—the needs of a husband, the commands of a boss, the demands of a child, the whines of a customer, the schedules of strangers.

We're bone-tired. There's no letup. We don't care about anyone or anything. We're afraid to risk and reluctant to want. We're embroiled in one constant, unrelenting emotion.

Or we're bored—life's not fast, fulfilling, or flowing with excitement.

We feel cramped, crowded, or cornered. There's too much activity and noise. We seem never to be alone. We hate our house. We're exhausted days and weeks on end. We scream more than we smile or laugh. We feel under the gun and over the edge. The house is a mess. We can't seem to keep the dust and grime out and the stuff in—inside the closets, hampers, drawers, and shelves.

Sounds like the mother of preschool children. Sounds like a woman juggling job and family. Sounds like a lot of us. Sounds like a potential runaway.

Along the freeways in the mountainous states, you'll see wonderful innovations—emergency ramps for out-of-control trucks. If one is barreling down a steep incline and the brake goes out, or the machinery gums up, or the driver flips out, he or she can veer off to a deep sand or gravel side road that slows and stops the runaway vehicle.

We need ramps like that—exits that help us regain control, side roads with a stopping place, not a straight-away to anywhere. Ramps with restraints.

We need time-outs.

Getaways

> Unlike the quick fix that alcohol, pills, drugs, or any other addictive escape may offer, play for the sake of play doesn't leave us with withdrawal symptoms.[1]

Temporary escapes refresh and renew the mind, body, and spirit while the heart stays home. Minivacations provide release from stress and pressure.

Sabbaticals, respites, R&R's rather than separation; giving notice, end of the chapter, termination—the former helps sift out whether the latter is the answer.

Karena has always been a housewife, a stay-at-home mom. That's all she's ever wanted to be. But she began to suspect that her family no longer needed her.

Her husband was absorbed in a career change. Two of her children were in college and came home on random weekends. The third had joined the marines.

She told her husband one morning at breakfast that she was going to leave home. "Just for awhile," she said, "to take a little trip." Her husband patted her on the back, pecked her cheek, and scooted out the door.

She talked with him about her proposed trip for several weeks. Then, one day after he left, she ran up the stairs and packed, grabbed some food she'd been stocking in the freezer and posted a note with instructions for her husband and the transient college kids.

"I drove over the state line and kept going. I stopped when I wanted. I rambled down any old road I took a notion to. I ate in restaurants and registered at motels alone for the first time in my life. But after a week of this, I got homesick.

"I was surprised when I returned. Only a few dishes were scattered in the sink; the laundry hamper was almost empty. Every can in the cupboard had been opened. There were messages on the answering machine for me . . . from all three kids, even the marine. 'I guess we were taking you for granted,' my husband said much later. Scrubbing the bathrooms didn't seem like such a lonely chore anymore, especially since I used that time to plan my next adventure. This time I talked my sister into going with me . . . clear to Houston!"

Karena is going to make her getaways a regular, scheduled priority.

We need a break when circumstances have become jumbled and confused or critical to the point of provoking a crisis. We need a release from life as usual.

Getaways provoke reality checks: I am *here!*

That is, when they help us unclutter our minds, when we stop "rushing after things, or running inside (ourselves)."[2] Our thoughts can run away, while we remain perfectly still. When they dart from one thing to another, without control or reason, without an observable outline, we must ask ourselves, "What am I thinking?" and write it all down or explain it to someone until someone understands. That's when we can set our minds to a plan of action: "I am going to do this. I am going to go here."

Getaways can be very private or crammed with people. They can be pure fun or serious bouts of meditation. When we feel the longing for a getaway, we need to determine what will get the job done.

Do we need a circle of sympathizers or a private chapel? Do we need a recreation room or a library? Do we need a jogging path or a quilt by a lakeside? Do we need solitude or companionship? Do we need one best friend or to be thrown into a crush of shoppers or a swarm of fans?

Anything will work that allows us to "briefly drop out of time, focus on the moment and lose ourselves in it . . . abandon ourselves to the possibility of delight at what is around us right now."[3]

Getaways smooth the handling of upheaval, disruptions, and rapid change. While some thrive on such excitement as the adrenaline flows, others panic. Some are energized, others are paralyzed.

When we want everything to stay the same, sudden change is upsetting. Gradual modifications are easier to accommodate, especially if explanations and reason are thrown in along the way. Dealing with stress requires might and muscle.

But crisis rarely comes unawares. Says psychotherapist Conalee Levine-Shneidman, "Nothing happens without warning. When something bad happens, you have to be mature about it. You have to ask yourself, 'What have I done to contribute to this?' Because it's a child's view of life that . . . you've contributed nothing and the other party contributed everything."[4]

Getaways are stepping out of a routine—to play or to think, to explore or to just be, to get a grip or understand what's going on.

A proper getaway can be: bouncing balloons, building sand castles, playing hide-and-seek, smiling at strangers, wiggling toes in warm sand or soft grass, getting a foot massage or manicure, watching falling rain or waterfalls or fountains, climbing a hill, kicking leaves, riding a bike, digging in a garden, playing cribbage, taking tap dance lessons, chatting with a neighbor, throwing a party, washing dishes by hand, drinking a chocolate mocha with whipped cream and grated chocolate curls—two hundred miles away from bossy phones, whines, and clocks.

Nature's daily pilgrimage provides simpler getaways, if we'll watch and listen: the hum of barbed wire on a windy day, a bee's buzz, a flock of birds chirping and flitting in a willow tree, a meteor blazing overhead, the trails on an ant hill, the shape of a fly's wing, the weave of a spider's web across a wall, a caterpillar inching across a busy road, dragonflies dancing at sunset.

Della desperately needed a getaway, but she didn't know how. She cared around the clock for her chronically ill husband. When she carefully thought over her schedule, she finally found her break: between midnight and 3:00 a.m. That's the only time when her husband, without fail, slept.

"I rearranged my habits so I could be awake and alert those hours. That was my time, to do what I wanted, without interruption. It so refreshed me that caring for my husband no longer seemed a burden, but a privilege."

To take time out to play does not mean we're atrophying, that we're not learning. Getting a break for housewife Joy Stubbs made her realize that her viewpoint about her family was a matter of "interpretation and mood. . . . I and I alone am responsible for how good or bad I feel. . . . When I am happy about myself, I feel needed."[5]

Music Therapy

On a tattered piece of paper tacked to an office door were found these words: "Music is God's best gift to man, the only art of heaven given to earth, the only art of earth we take to heaven."

Certain kinds of music can make us edgy; others fill us with peace. Music can agitate us, or cause our souls to soar.

Singing in the shower, harmonizing in the car, humming along with friends, attacking a piano, hymns and choruses on Sunday morning, a concert Friday night, soothing sounds from the radio alarm at dawn—music is medicine. Music is communication to and from our inward beings. Music can be praise and worship to God.

When an evil spirit tormented King Saul, his attendants recommended that David, the shepherd boy, play his harp to soothe him. Saul would not only feel better when David came to play, but the evil spirit would actually leave him (1 Samuel 16:14–23).

Today studies show that the right kind of music helps "reduce stress and chronic pain, lower blood pressure, boost the immune response, and reduce depression and incidents of insomnia. . . it touches us on a physical, a psychological, and a spiritual level."[6] Music affects the brain, either as a sedative or a stimulant.

Music washes our environment, stirs our senses, lifts us out of ourselves. Music is the perfect complement for a getaway.

The Lost Art of Letter Writing

Another way to relieve tensions is to spill it all out on paper—to a soul mate, or to ourselves. Women in generations past discovered ways "to help each other explore the events and patterns in their lives"[7] through long years of expansive letter writing. We rarely make the effort—to our great loss.

> Letters are magical. I never throw out a good letter . . . . Letters document the chapters in our lives—our discoveries, our passions, our sorrows and growth as

well as all the ebb and flow inevitable in life . . . the most accurate and natural form of autobiography.[8]

A meaningful letter not only tells what's happening to us now, but also recalls events in the past and how they made us feel. We record what matters most to us and to the people with whom we're communicating. We disclose an inner part of us. Letters, journals, and diaries provide a way to talk through our desires and reasons for running away—without actually running. When we sort and outline and organize our thoughts *out there* in the light where we can see them, rather than hide them inside where they stay shadowy, dark, puzzling— we can set our minds to a plan of action: "I will do this. I will go there. I will say that."

Even coffee or lunch with a friend slows down panic, releases immediate pressures to enable more constructive and clear minded thinking.

Litter Control

We sweat to fight the clutter—the stuff, the ill-arranged stuff, the unwanted stuff, the sentimental stuff, the vital, valuable, absolutely precious stuff. And the bigger the barn we own, the more hay we cram in.

My friend and I will drive along a scenic route and spot a lovely, sprawling ranch house. I see rooms begging to be decorated. She sees billions of thingies to be vacuumed. "H-work," she calls it.

Housework deluges us, especially when everything else is out of whack. But it changes our attitude when we improve our surroundings. Cleaning an entire room, washing all the windows, dusting the treasures on the shelf, setting the radio or tape player close by where we'll really use it, purchasing decorative plants—these simple steps put us in motion, get our minds off whining, and may actually produce an appreciative comment or two.

> To take housework seriously means that the person
> sees what needs doing, thinks about it, plans how to
> resolve problems connected with it, and then takes the
> necessary time out of the work day to make sure it gets
> done.[9]

Cleaning house is the most necessary, frustrating, never ending duty on this earth. It never gets done. It needs doing every day. An hour later, it screams for attention again. The frustration level mounts according to the number of persons encamped in the house per square foot, their ages, and their cooperation.

The closest scene to heaven on this earth is one's own house scrubbed top to bottom until it sparkles, done by a cleaning service. The nearest thing to an angel is a willing, faithful, competent, affordable housekeeper.

Most homemakers receive little feedback regarding the quality of their work, no salary for compensation, no reward for duties completed; and they often confront a family's unrealistic expectations and daily demands.

For those who care for a house, satisfaction levels increase with cooperation and caring—clearly communicated directions and a sense of team spirit. Housework, however, is usually done alone.

We all have those particular tasks that threaten to unglue us. For some, it's meal planning. We really don't mind cooking. It's just the time and energy required to constantly think up delectable delights, three times a day, every day. If someone would just say, "We want chicken pot pie," or "How about salmon steaks this week?" we're just fine. Meanwhile, we stare with frustration into the cupboards a half hour before mealtime.

Ironing, recycling, overflowing closets. We want to run. Instead we can take a break, then attack them with renewed vigor. Sometimes the most courageous thing we can do is, by an act of the will, place one foot in front of the other and keep to our appointed rounds.

An old Chinese proverb says, "A hundred men may make an encampment, but it takes a woman to make a home." That's the pity. That's the glory.

Swapping—for a Day

Comedian Joan Rivers discovered an inventive way to see one's life from a fresh perspective. She traded her designer clothes for a Denny's uniform in West Palm Beach, Florida, and worked third shift for a waitress who won Rivers' Life Swap contest. Rhonda Denton was the winner, based on Rivers' review of entrants' videotapes. She got to play host on Rivers' talk show on March 4, 1994. We can try this too—but only temporarily.

Amusing Grace . . . How Sweet the Sound of Laughter[10]

A smile lifts the face and the spirit. Lining our situation with a cup of cheer creates a whole new texture. Author Barbara Johnson tells how she does it.

> I searched for a word to describe all the STUFF that can happen to us. Words like *problems, troubles,* or *tragedies* just didn't cut it because they were too grim. But then I found it—gloomees . . . it's hard to say 'gloomees' without at least a hint of a smile.[11]

When we laugh the brain secretes chemicals called endorphins, which stimulate healing throughout the body. We're playing nurse and doctor as much as mother and grandparent when we wiggle our noses, make silly faces, bug our eyes, and speak in squeaky voices until a baby giggles. Too bad we don't have our personal jesters, like the kings and queens of old.

We can try to turn the events of our days into reasons for laughter. Seen from the right perspective, so much in our lives is whimsical. Says educator Sara Lawrence Lightfoot,

> [Learning] is at its best when it's deadly serious and very playful at the same time. . . in every serious thought, there's a line of laughter.[12]

Balance is beautiful—when there's passion and play, discipline and humor, absolutes and feeling.

Getaways are very different from running away, or moving on.

Moving On

Like running away, to move on is a permanent kind of leave-taking, but the situation or relationship has amicable transition and closure through communication and agreement. All parties involved know what's going on, when, and why. There's harmony and commitment to continued communication and caring for those left behind. Moving on integrates a series of positive actions and decisions and results in a spurt of growth in character, hope, and healing for the individual. She steps into the next stage of her life journey.

Moving on, as well as announced and approved getaways, prevent the shock, pain, and rage that's so difficult to heal when hard-earned trust is undermined.

Moving on could be starting a career, or getting a degree. It could be getting a life, or even taking a flight to safety. In a sense, we should always be moving on—exploring ideas, experimenting with solutions, entering new passages, learning lessons—"Forgetting what is behind and straining toward what is ahead" (Philippians 3:13).

When a Woman Needs a Solution

Cultivating good habits, disciplines, and rhythms to our daily lives soothes the spirit, rejuvenates the body, and removes the guilt and tension.[13]

Jan needed more than a break. She required a complete overhaul. She was on overload.

A couple walking their dog stopped to visit with her as she sat alone in her car in a parking lot. They politely asked, "How are you?" and she burst into sobs. "What's the matter?" they asked, greatly alarmed.

"I've got to quit. It's too much."

Thinking she was talking about a board they served on together, they assured her, "We'll take care of your part of the business at the next meeting. You get a rest. You're doing such a good job."

"No! That's not what I mean. If I don't get some help right away, I'm checking myself into a mental hospital."

It was more than one board meeting that threatened to do her in. At church she was president of the women's association and clerk of the session and Bible study leader. In the community she was on call twenty-four hours a day as an emergency medical technician, treasurer of the fire department, community center committee president, in charge of the city's recycling, a member of the city council, secretary of the city park committee, voting registrar, as well as friend and neighbor to many, and a wife, mother, and sister.

"These all took much time and discipline and energy. So, when I faced a rash of criticism, a clash with a close friend and some devastating family news—all within a few days—I had no reserves left. I crashed. I can see now it had been coming on for a long time."

She quit everything. She stayed at home, spent months of long, quiet hours in study, prayer, and meditation.

When the body quits, emotions shut down, pain throbs, and all we can see is clouds of confusion, it's time to come to a complete stop. It's time to scale down.

"I dropped one class because I was overloaded, and I feel *much* better now," my sister, Connie, wrote recently. "I knew that would be a problem when I signed up, but hoped I could keep up. Am thankful for the fact I listen to my body and don't try to be Super Person."

Simple time management suggestions clear a space in our schedules and relieve feelings of being overwhelmed. Practical helps prevent desperation and ease burdens. Cherie Collister tells of a woman overcome with loneliness and uselessness in a foreign culture, and tempted to run back to the familiar.

"A Chinese-speaking mother felt isolated in the middle of a huge city. She was kept home indefinitely by the needs of her premature baby. All her relatives live in Taiwan. Her husband is a typical Silicon Valley guy working fourteen to sixteen hours a day and in constant fear of a layoff. Her culture tells her that if her baby is 'sick,' it is her fault. So, she's piled with guilt and insecurity.

"She wanted desperately to go back to school and acquire some job skills, but her English was too poor. So, I helped her negotiate the bureaucracy of the community college. When she fretted that she wouldn't have time to go to an ESL (English as a Second Language) class, I pointed out that the length of the class was about the same as a trip to the grocery store. The outing then looked more achievable. She enrolled in the class and finally made some friends."

Lessons from Running

"The sorriest memory of my high school days proved to be the best preventive for quitting in tough times as an adult," Macy told me.

"My senior year I was a starter on the girls' basketball team. Towards the end of the season, just before district playoffs, I quit the team. I wanted more time with my boyfriend. I was tired of the stress of the games. I wasn't getting along with one of the other girls. All these reasons seemed compelling at the time.

"A few weeks later our team went to the state finals and won the state championship. Every time I visit my old high school gym, my name's not on the permanent banner hung on the wall . . . a painful reminder. I've regretted the decision ever since. Since then, I've been working on my tendency to be negative under pressure, and tried to develop better coping skills."

Macy has three highschoolers of her own now. "All three are active in sports. I tell them, 'You don't have to go out for the team, but once you commit, you stay to the end of the season.' My daughter told me that as she goes from one game to the next, she tries to erase the previous game. It's done and over and she keeps going on to the next play. I'm proud she's not a quitter."

Barbara Jo is a single woman who chased one job after another because of the fear of failure. After careful assessment of where her career was going, she determined to stay at her next job, no matter what, at least two years. She's been there five years now. "I made it through all the stages where I used to freak out before by sheerly sticking with the original goal I set for myself" she explains. "The two years drug on like a lifetime. Now, it seems like nothing."

We spend so much time and energy trying to escape from the heat and fire of troubles. That usually means running from people or challenge or accomplishment. Often the events we think will diminish us turn out to be our greatest boon and fulfillment.

Adversity reveals truth—of who we are, who we aren't; of what we can take, what we can't; of who's with us and who's against us. Misfortune humbles us when we believe our world's under our tight control. Distress teaches us compassion for others who are harassed and harried. Persevering through trials cures indecision, double-mindedness, and hypocrisy. Running away from our choices can stall the progress, prolong the process. Certain kinds of running stunt growth. Getaways keep us plugging through. That is, the right kinds.

A mother left her three young children, ages six to eleven, alone for a week, in hopes of a getaway. She told them she'd be back, and she was, only to face charges of three counts of injury to a child, a misdemeanor. Police found an unkempt house with dirty dishes covering the stove and little more than milk, cheese, and hot dogs in the refrigerator. The oldest child said her mother had left like this several times before.[14]

When is a getaway actually a runaway?

A Sanctuary

A woman in Dedham, Massachusetts lives in a large, rambling house with her husband and children—but maintains a small apartment in a nearby town. "It's my sanctuary, a place I can run to when things pile up too much for me at home," she explains.[15]

The church should be a refuge—a haven of rejuvenation and rest. The church is not only a pool for spiritual resources, a prod for spiritual disciplines, but also a family. God is forming a family out of strangers—to purge personal demons and hug runaways home.

Every age produces those who find appeal in the convent life, for those who "have only one desire and this is the desire for solitude—to disappear into God . . . solitude [as a] vocation, not as flight from the world, but as [a] place in the world."[16]

A convent provides order, rhythm, routine, communal activity. But a retreat is a place of rest in order to nourish the spirit and soul. It's a place of discovery, to better know God, to learn how to do ourselves and others the most good.

Marcella, a wealthy Italian woman who lived in the fourth century, founded the first religious community for women. She turned her "sumptuous palace on the Aventine in Rome into a Christian retreat."[17]

Kitty Dukakis, a recovering alcoholic, counsels others with alcoholism. She interned three days a week at Wayside House of Delray Beach, Florida, a twenty-four-bed nonprofit center for women addicted to drugs or alcohol.

"I think I could have gotten sober at Wayside," she said, adding she doesn't think most people can kick bad habits on their own. "Some people can do it, but it's much more difficult."[18]

We need some sort of shepherding homes for women in limbo or crisis, with trained staff personnel, both paid and volunteer, who would be willing to go where the woman is, if need be, to talk with her in her home, at her church, at a local restaurant. Publicity would help, letting women know about the support and help available from a resource like this, communicating who and where it is. Focus would be needed—to understand the goals of the group and understand a wide spectrum of women's problems. A major problem would be, of course, funding.

In the Old Testament we learn of entire towns that were set aside as "cities of refuge." These were places those accused of murder could flee to for protection from the victim's family and friends as they pleaded their case for involuntary homicide, or were "released from banishment by the death of the high priest."[19]

Kathleen Fuller of Destin, Florida, helps heal the wounds of life in her own small way. She rents her harbor cottage to people who need a place "to relax and soak in the beauty of God's creation." She named her cottage The Hiding Place.[20]

A refuge. A place of protection and immunity. A community of faith. Women who want to run need a shelter like this while they're sorting things out, while they determine which way to go next.

Psalm 39:5 reminds us, "Truly every man at his best is merely a breath!" (AMPLIFIED).

"How did I get here so soon?" the eighty-six-year-old woman at the convalescent home calls out to no one in particular.

Life is brief, over too soon. Yet, sometimes our trials threaten to go on forever.

We all need breaks, sometimes, from the routines and ruts and ravages, when the mind's locked up, when we're squeezed, when too much is happening, when God seems far away.

We can grasp a piece of time by slowing down, unjumbling our thoughts, sliding into a Jacuzzi, by getting away.

Discovery Questions

1. Dr. Harold Sala, in his booklet *Boredom and How to Overcome It*, says, "Goals that are absolutely impossible are worse than no goals at all because to fail to reach them only frustrates you the more."[21]
   What do you hope to accomplish today?
   This week?
   By the end of next month?
   Within a year?
   Five years from now?

2. Do you consider yourself a valued person?
   What makes you feel this way?

3. What do you really enjoy doing?
   What makes you feel most productive?
   What activities drain you?
   What causes you to feel spiritually refreshed?

4. What is one change in your daily routine you could make, starting tomorrow, that would greatly relieve stress?

5. Which scene best describes, as you understand it, the purpose or reality of this life:
   A Disneyland? A recess? A horse race? A boot camp? A school room? A boxing match? A ballroom?

A deserted island? A stock market crash? A rat race? A pleasure cruise? A parenthesis? A roller coaster? A hall of crazy mirrors? A relay race? A graveyard? A ride on a bucking bull? A shuffleboard game?

Explain your answer.

6. If you were free tomorrow to do anything or go anywhere with anyone you wanted, what would you choose?

Why can't you do that?

7. Read Mark 4:35–41, 6:30–32, 45–46.
    When, how, and why did Jesus take breaks?

8. Give two examples of what you consider a clear-cut case of moving on, rather than running away, one from contemporary examples and one from the Bible.

9. Changes in which of these situations do you think would most improve the quality of a woman's life?

Juggling career and mothering; lack of adequate childcare; husbands who help little or not at all; little or no leisure time; siblings uninvolved in care of elderly parents; broken families; no designated lines of family obligation; young, unmarried motherhood; no financial security; incomplete education; no partner to share burden of responsibility.

Explain your answer.

Notes

[1]Joyce Brothers, "Do You Have Enough Fun?" *Parade*, 2 February 1992, 4.

[2]de Waal, *Journey with Thomas Merton*, 92.

[3]Brothers, "Do You Have Enough Fun?" 4.

[4]Conalee Levine-Schneidman, interview by Alice Kosner, "Making the Best of Change," *Cosmopolitan*, February 1992, 68.

[5]Joy Stubbs, "I Was a Runaway Wife . . . Who Went Home," *Ladies Home Journal*, September 1980, 18.

[6]Lisa Dionne, "Good Vibrations," *Aspire*, April/May 1995, 40, 42.

[7]Leslie A. Moushey, "The Search for Identity," *Belles Lettres* (Summer 1989): 9.

[8]Alexandra Stoddard, *Gift of a Letter* (New York: Avon, 1990), 6.

[9]Braverman, "The Dilemma of Housework," 28.

[10]Johnson, *Pack Up Your Gloomees*, 235.

[11]Ibid., 4.

[12]*A World of Ideas*, 156.

[13]Newenhuyse, *I Feel Like Running Away*, 44.

[14]Associated Press, "Mother Accused of Leaving Three Kids for a Week," *Lewiston* (Idaho) *Morning Tribune*, 17 February 1995, C3.

[15]Brenton, *The Runaways*, 3–4.

[16]de Waal, *Journey with Thomas Merton*, 27.

[17]Edith Deen, *Great Women of the Christian Faith* (Westwood, N.J.: Barbour, 1959), 17.

[18]Kitty Dukakis, interviewed by Associated Press, *Lewiston* (Idaho) *Morning Tribune*, 23 January 1992, A6.

[19]*Peloubet's Bible Dictionary*, ed. F. N. Peloubet and Alice D. Adams (Philadelphia: Universal Book and Bible House, 1947), 121.

[20]Fish, "Caught between Expectations," 17.

[21]Harold Sala, *Boredom and How to Overcome It*.

Ten

Life Choices in a Sensual, Material, Runaway World
Curbing the Urge to Run: Part Two

If we could live our lives over again, what would we change? Less time with what? More time with whom? What scenes would we edit? What decisions would we nix?

Running away is rarely the original folly. A runaway may be reaping the outcome of earlier, unwise choices—such as substance abuse, bad partnerships, criminal activity, taking one of various kinds of risks (with health or safety), and poor money management. This chapter focuses on three main life choices for a woman—sex, marriage, and parenting—and how our thinking about ourselves and God affects the decisions we make.

Getting a Grip on Sex

A woman relates to her world in four main ways: intellectually, emotionally, sensually, and spiritually. One of these may be dominant. When the emotional and sensual throbs out of control, we're deaf, blind, and foolish. We detonate our ability to make good choices.

What would we do differently, given our state of mind today? Michele Halseide writes, "Although my mother says she would spend less time housekeeping and more time playing with her children, other women tell me they would say no to premarital sex, marry someone else, or not marry at all."[1]

The things we would want to change often deal with repercussions that led to lack of control, lack of choices later down the line; the actions that meant depleted resources, soured relationships, spurned opportunities.

"We enjoyed visits over the fence, just about every weekend," explains Bree. "We talked about all kinds of things. It was refreshing to be able to talk to a man so easily. We were becoming fast friends. Then, slowly, the conversations began to get a bit suggestive. I sensed a red flag waving. I knew I needed to back off. I waited to visit, after that, until one of the kids or my husband was in the yard too. We remained friends, but only that."

How perfect our days would be if all our relationships were right ones, healthy ones, ones that enabled us to grow and be and do all that God purposed when He created us. If only we could find the control over our minds and hearts and wills, coupled with heavenly wisdom, always to make the right choices, to stay within safe bounds, never to hurt or be stung. If we could always sense the warning signs, see the red flag waving over the beginning of a wrong choice, a bad turn, and make the needed detour or stop in our tracks or do the right kind of running. If only we had control.

Sexual abstinence, except in marriage, means freedom. No forced pregnancies or premature emotional and physical entanglements. No diseases or risks for a one night stand. No being used and leaving a part of yourself with every guy who comes along. No perversions of your self-image. No diving in heart first. Saying no means saying yes to a clear conscience, a free spirit, feet firmly on the ground, and lots of options.

At different seasons of our lives, we must determine whether we'll be governed by runaway hormones or reasoned restraints, whether we choose our partners by sex appeal or the proven test of developing compatible companionship. Sex, too soon and too intense, consumes us, to the exclusion of discernment and reason.

Patti describes her experience. "My days were full of good things—well-paying job, supportive family, excellent health—but all I could think about was plotting to enjoy those few moments of passion. It was like some kind of addiction. I needed a get-away . . . to sort out what was right for me, away from the drugging influence of those touches."

Abstinence means power for a woman, control over her life that allows her to keep making choices. It's not just a physical experience, like jogging or fast dancing. We set in motion all sorts of other parts of us, the total person. We commit our spirits, our affections, our wills, our self-image to this other person. We can't play games with this drive without losing much more than we gain. With the right partner, who will affirm us in our sexuality, while allowing us to stay in charge, we can avoid the aftershock of deep regret and pain.

But we're sensitized people plunked down in a sensual society. We need to be taught what to resist and how to say no. We've got to understand the role God purposed for sex.

We can't flip on the TV more than a few seconds without encountering sexual innuendoes or blatant sexual poses. There's sex in advertising, sex in the movies, sex on the magazine racks, sex in the bestsellers, sex in the newspapers, sex in music, sex on videos, sex in the malls and the halls, sex in politics, sex when you least expect it and anytime you want it. No longer considered sacred and precious and exclusive, sex is trivialized and merchandised and overemphasized.

"Take me to a nunnery," we want to cry at times, "where I can be surrounded by pure things, lovely things, something other than sex things."

Even in the best of situations—loving, wholesome family relationships, stable childhoods, controlled courtships—the mass production of sexual distortion threatens to influence our minds and actions. But how many have experienced the best of situations?

Complications abound when we're cut down in our defenses by incest, by abuse, by rape, by violence, by rejection. The longing for love and acceptance and affirmation can thrust us into the deadend of sexual union. We join bodies, without becoming friends. We grab a brief thrill, ignoring the long-play pleasures of sharing hopes and dreams and goals and interests and skills. Then, if we're not dumped, we're stuck in the relationship, trying to squeeze some depth from a bond that never was given a chance to grow.

Bonds That Empower, Bonds That Endure

There are no perfect men. But we want to find the right one for us. Most of us make this choice when we're young—hormones raging, emotions still wet behind the tears, insecurities so strong we're hardly aware of what we believe or what we want except that it's cool to catch a man, who is probably very much a boy.

Marriage is the ultimate, permanent invasion of privacy. It's also meant to be a protective barrier against the world. It's a bond that can soften the blows of reality, while giving a good dose of it.

> Even in an era when marriage is often a fragile arrangement between couples, its capacity to protect people from the full impact of external strains makes it a surprisingly stable social institution.[2]

In marriage, problems and pleasures are shared, someone cares about us and we have someone to care about. Marriage satisfies our hunger for intimacy when "we want to be able to relax our guard with someone else, to feel known and cared about, warts and all, without having to be afraid of rejection."[3]

Choosing a compatible counterpart, a companionable marriage partner, is crucial to avoiding the need to run away. A reasonable length of courtship, the process of dating and interacting provides an opportunity to see this potential life mate under a variety of circumstances and determine whether companionship, as well as chemistry, holds on with positive, steady growth.

Questions we should ask ourselves and our future partner before we marry:

• Do we have at least five shared interests or similarities?

• How are we different? How important are these differences? Are they complementary, or could they create chaos?

• What are our spiritual commitments? Beliefs?

• How many compromises must I make to commit to this relationship?

• What major problems must we solve?

• Does this person have a pattern of making poor choices?

• Have we weathered any crises together? How did we handle them?

• Can I continue to love this one, without any changes?

• What do I enjoy most about this person? Least?

• Are we good friends?

• Do significant people in my life agree that we're good for each other?

• Do we have moments of joy and shared laughter?

• What benefits does this person add to my life?

• Have I met all the important people in this person's life? Are we compatible?

• What are this person's family behavior patterns? Is this comforting, or troubling?

• Are we able to talk about deeply personal subjects?

• How do we deal with anger?

• Do we know each other's moods?

• Who will handle the finances?

• If this person walked out of my life right now, what would I feel: relief, or a gaping hole of loss?

Some lawmakers have gone so far as to suggest that we impose a waiting period for marriage licenses. In the state of Washington a bill was introduced that would require licenses to come with "warnings about spousal abuse." Says Washington state senator, Margarita Prentice, "I would say, simply, beware. Stop, look, listen and be cautious. Marriage is serious business."[4]

Ben Franklin wisely said, "Keep your eyes wide open before marriage, half shut afterwards."

But the Bible also warns, "Marriage should be honored by all" (Hebrews 13:4).

Marriage is honored by staying sexually faithful to our spouse, by doing all we can to learn to be a friend and helping partner and lover to this one man. This is a fine tuned art that takes much practice—a sturdy, life-long challenge for any woman.

We can expect several seasons in matrimony: romance, casual irritation, total disillusionment, revival of romance.

"It sounds absurdly simple, but doing more of what works in the marriage and less of what doesn't is the key," says Michele Weiner-Davis, one of an increasing number of marital therapists who believe divorce simply doesn't work. "Focus on what has worked, the things you used to do when you felt loving, and do them again. The action helps trigger the feelings."[5]

A change in our behavior produces a change in his. Change something—a predictable pattern, a ritual, a habit. Behave in the opposite way. One person can cause change.

"I was totally at the end of my resources," LaDonna told me. "He refused to take care of his health, try to keep a job, or to take care of me and the kids. My naggings, threats, and carefully explained harangues accomplished nothing. So, I searched for something—anything—to appreciate him for, to show my thanks, to try to nurture back that love we once had. I did a 180—the exact reverse of what I'd been doing. He slowly responded. I realized I'd been beating down his fragile ego with my blaming. He had felt like a failure, all shaky inside, and so stopped trying. He desperately needed my support, not my searing slings."

When marital bliss diminishes to hanging on for survival, we wonder if the joy is gone forever. Our union is no longer secure, ordered, predictable, controllable. Perhaps the entire ground of our relationship is being plowed. If so, a surprise development may be in store. But the process can be unpleasant, disconcerting. Some run before the flowering.

No man can fulfill our every need. No human can do that. Only God can. The imperfect man we marry has needs and wounds and pride of his own to overcome. He has ambitions to reach. He, too, may have a lot to learn about lifetime loving. Marriage is the ultimate training course in practicing the art of managing relationships.

The most important attitude one can have toward her husband is *contentment*, a renewed satisfaction, after all the warts and blemishes have been exposed, to have chosen this man above all others as one's life partner. No more unfavorable comparisons. No more trying to completely overhaul him. Just relishing the pure joy of who he is, rather than who he is not. A woman must make peace with her selection.

The highest grace we can bestow on our mate is *courtesy*, the public respect and private attentiveness to his opinions, ideas, and dreams. We practice the basics of manners—"please" and "thank you" and "how are you really, today?"

As we face disappointment and disillusionment, the best gift we can incorporate into the fabric of our marriage is *courage*—that word of hope, actions of help, willingness to try once more, to see what another day will bring. We face the bills another month. We encourage him in his job. We praise his attempts at fathering. We tell him what we appreciate about his lovemaking. We try to understand his struggles to communicate.

Finally, the best characteristic we can invest in this plum of relationships is *creativity*. The same passion and energy and ingenuity we'd give to our dream career we measure out right in our home.[6]

There's a flow in every relationship—ups and downs, ins and outs, quiet pleasures and times of intense dislike as we gradually get to know each other. If we handle each other with care and respect as we expose our inner selves we soon begin to feel understood and safe with each other as we weather the storms. Ultimate healing nearly always comes from a loving, intimate relationship. But strident kinships can reach a fever pitch that drives us to the nearest exit. We've got to survive, any way we can. Or we stay, and flex coping muscles we never knew we had.

"I wish we'd had a counselor, a mediator, years ago in our marriage," says Elaine Nelson Thompson, "who could help us communicate our needs to each other, keep us from hurting each other. We had problems, serious ones, right from the beginning. Our relationship started all wrong. We both had deep emotional needs. Now it's too late. I ran and we're all paying a terrible price."

A good marriage softens and undergirds the creaks and strains of parenting and making one's way in a hostile or apathetic world. Working on a marriage relationship is the most necessary, infuriating—and at the same time satisfying—exercise anyone can undertake. That promise we made to each other can pull us through black spells when our anguish or anger tempts us to pull out.

"We're friends forever, no matter what," say the two young girls as they make a pact in a tree house. Years later one runs to the side of the other as she lays ill, to care for her kids and cook her meals.

"We're husband and wife forever, no matter what," say two novices at an altar. The years bring change and choices and our terrible freedom. We can run if we want. Or we can try to make the promise work.

Conflict management courses should be required in school. We can't escape conflict—power struggles, personality clashes, ego duels, miscues. Competent referees or mediators provide peace, thoughtful pauses, or insight and solutions when we don't know what to do next.

The best counseling classes instruct couples "on the principles that make relationships wholesome and happy, and equip them with the biblical skills of mercy, grace, and forgiveness that will take them through tough times."[7]

Then Come Kids

When are we best prepared to be mothers?

What's the right timing? How many can we handle? Is the emotional, financial, and marital climate ready?

Having kids is a major life choice.

Becoming a mother is to enter the most mysterious commitment life has to offer. Like a game of Russian roulette, we reach out for a surprise package. We never know what or who we're going to get. Once they're here, we're forever Mom—for better or worse.

A person (or persons) invades our world. We're attached, we're involved. We're entwined in a lifetime challenge of getting to know each other, making as few mistakes as possible, of constant change and trying to get it right for this one and starting all over with the next one.

Even if we do everything by the book, this child has a mind and will of her own. Kids make their own choices, and that reflects back on us. They become an extension of us, yet separate. They're our kids, yet he's his own man. They're our responsibility, yet she's her own woman.

Children bring perplexity and promise. They bring confusion and the sweet smile of peace. They're baggage and burden and blessing for the woman who wants or needs to run.

The Way We Think

Three pastors were visiting one day and discussing their congregations. The first one said his people reminded him of a swarm of fleas. They were always crowding around him. The second one said his people were like alley cats, always fighting about one thing or another. The third replied, after a moment of reflection, "Our members are like a basket of mending. So many needs, so little time."

The churches were very much alike, but each of the shepherds perceived the individuals in very different ways, according to their personalities, spiritual gifts, and insights.

In the same way, we see our relationships, our situations and ourselves according to emotional and experiential and knowledge filters.

Do we know who we truly are?

Do we know what God thinks of us?

How we see ourselves, what we perceive of God, largely determines the choices we entertain, the decisions we make. Our personal identity grows through our associations, our encounters, and by cultivation.

We claim our identity in many ways:

- whose daughter?
- whose wife?
- whose mother?
- what career?
- where born?
- where raised?
- what education?
- what talents?
- what interests?
- what beliefs?

Some of these identities we choose for ourselves. Others are appointed for us. Our true identity is an integrated combination of all we used to be, and all we are now, and what we're hoping to become. Each of us is a unique combination.

We can temporarily lose our identity, as when shaken loose from a job, or key relationship, or geographical roots. Then, we can struggle to know who we are again. We grope for meaning when a part of our foundation, our definition, has been taken away.

We can temporarily lose our identity when pressed into mobs of people. Prolonged anonymity can diminish us. Citizens of megacities feel this. So do prisoners in jails and war camps. So do refugees and the homeless. We become numbers, members of a faceless throng pulled into an impersonal, teeming mass.

We can try to hide our identity—by pretense, by practice, by neglect, or by running away. How do we know if we're running away from who we are? Here are some clues:

• Not one of our closest friends knows any significant details about the first eighteen years of our lives.

• We would never, ever use our maiden name to fill out a public form—like signing checks, on stationery, or the cover of our latest book.

• We cringe when someone introduces us as "one of the Chester kids," "the girl who used to live on Rinaldi Street," or "our pastor's wife."

• When asked, "What do you do?" we answer, "Oh, I'm just a housewife," or we beef up our job description in a way that would make our boss laugh.

• We rarely wear our wedding ring, though it still fits.

• When certain family members suddenly enter our office, school, or meeting room, we avoid introducing them to our coworkers or friends.

• When the leader of a group asks everyone to state her name, where she's from, and one interesting fact about herself, we sweat great drops while waiting our turn, then excuse ourselves to the bathroom or hall while our neighbor replies for us.

We all have times when we don't expose our full identities; depending on the environment, the people we're with, the mood we're in, our purpose at the time, the appropriateness of the disclosure. Key considerations are:

• Our inner motivations

  Is it because of tact or ignorance?

  Is it because of discretion or fear?

  Is it because of humility or shame?

• Our habitual response

Was this a momentary lapse, or a necessary exception, or do we always get jittery about this personal subject? Self-dissatisfaction is usually what prompts a desire to escape a present reality. But any running away—whether in the form of abusing drugs, alcohol, or through desertion—"merely drives the individual into deeper self-dissatisfaction."[8]

We need loving, caring groups and individuals, such as those found in churches, to draw us out, to help affirm our tentative knowledge of ourselves.

Christy used to think she was hollow inside. She was afraid to be too introspective because if she looked very far, she might really find nothing there. But as she participated in a Bible study, and found friendships there, she found a process of affirmation. As she talked to others, they told her the good things they saw in her and the capabilities she had.

One of her friends says, "I remember my surprise when Christy said she felt inferior. I shared my reaction with her. She has an ability to think and to speak her thoughts, an ability I admire. But I had never told her that because I thought she knew what a fantastic mind she has."

Through feedback like this, Christy discovered who she is. It's refreshing to her that other people can know her and still like her.[9]

Running-away behavior grows out of a woman's thinking she's all alone, a sense that everything's against her. She becomes isolated and feels insecure. She's vulnerable to making poor choices.

The mind is where it's at. What we put in there—what we see and read and listen to and, therefore, choose to believe—those are the resources for making our decisions, for determining what action we'll take.

How can we know when we're in our right mind?

When we're in our right mind, we have determined who and where and what is our home. We know where we belong. We have problems, but we keep seeking help. We have more problems, but we're learning how to handle them and how to behave under the stress. We find a vision of what we should accomplish, what's really important, and we never let go.

When we're *not* in our right mind we're lost in a sea of despond, an ocean of despair without a trickle of hope.

When we think of a runaway, what state of mind do we picture? Easily unsettled? Alarmed? Skittish? Unstable? Steered by impulse? Or do we imagine her engaged in deep, meditative thought? Is she alone, stuffed in her narrow box of limited information? Or is she surrounded by a great crowd of advisors?

When we think of a runaway, do we sense a person seeking after wisdom?

Wisdom is the gift Solomon asked for—the ability that enables one to know the right thing to do under any situation.

Wisdom is discernment followed by a course of action.

Wisdom is good, practical judgment, common sense, the ability to reason through to a wise conclusion.

Wisdom works the best moral ends for all persons involved.

Wisdom is appointed by inspiration for a given circumstance or cultivated through a long series of life experiences.

Wisdom most often comes through hindsight. For instance, "In order to do things differently, I would have to know *then* what I know *now.*"

The pursuit of wisdom is the highest challenge to the human mind and heart.

True wisdom belongs only to God.

Wisdom is peering through the smoke screen of chaos right into the core, the cause, the central irritant.

Sometimes we run because something or someone got out of control, and we panic.

In the field of science, researchers in the laboratory have learned to control the chaotic behavior of paper-thin metal ribbons, "simply by making small adjustments to one of the parameters governing the system's behavior." They have discovered that small disturbances radically alter behavior. Conversely, tiny adjustments can also stabilize behavior.

The process can be used in a wide variety of ways—from designing quieter submarines to patterning rapid adjustment pacemakers for heart patients. All they need to do is observe a system long enough to map its chaotic attractor and determine by experiments what brings it under control.[10]

By the penetrating insight of God's wisdom we can know the actions and prayers and words that can still small disturbances in people and situations that produce unruly behavior. We can make the adjustments that establish stability. It may take a while, but if we observe long enough and seek diligently enough and pray earnestly enough, control *in* chaos will come.

In the meantime, we can do what Marsha does. She has a habit of telling herself, out loud, during times of immense disorder, "I will not run! I will not run! I will not run—no matter what!" She says it does wonders for her backbone.

It takes courage to be a decisive woman. It takes boldness to be a wife. It takes grit to risk becoming a mother. And such ventures profoundly affect the rest of our lives.

Sex and marriage and kids: they're thrilling. They're also frightening. It's commitment.

Some women need identity. Some need hope. Some need help. Some need healing.

But we all need the wisdom of God.

Discovery Questions

1. Why is sexual immorality such a problem in our society? What, if anything, can we do about it?

What are some ways a young girl/woman today can stay out of sexually tempting situations?

2. How do you perceive marriage? As a dissolvable contract between two people? As a sacred commitment between two people and God? Comments:

What is one thing we could do to help make marriage stronger?

3. Think of a woman you know who is single, and content in her singleness. What is the reason for her contentment?

4. Read 1 Peter 2:25–3:6.
   Who is God to us?
   Who are we to be to our husbands? How do you feel about that?
   What things are important to God?
   If you are married, what is one practical thing you could do to improve your marriage relationship?

5. Read Luke 15:11–20.
   What did it take for the prodigal son to come to his senses, that is, to be in his right mind?

Do you know where your home is? Are you there right now? If not, why not?

6. What is the process you use to find wisdom?

7. Which is the best way to deal with a temptation? Find Scripture verses that will guide you.
   - think it all through
   - pray about it
   - discuss it with a trusted friend
   - run from the source
   - other:

8. Write down a brief description of who you are.

   Is any area of your identity or background difficult for you to acknowledge? Why?

9. Use a separate piece of paper for each for these topics: (a) family, (b) organizations, (c) finances, (d) politics, (e) career, (f) religion.
   Under each topic complete the sentences:
   "I was . . .," "I am . . .," "I hope to be . . ."

10. What do you think these verses tell us about identity?
    Isaiah 38:10–19
    1 John 4:7–12
    Romans 5:6–11
    Galatians 3:26–29
    1 Corinthians 12:4–31

Notes

[1]Michele Halseide, "If Only I Had . . . ," *Today's Christian Woman*, March/April 1992, 38.

[2]Gove, Style, and Hughes, "Effect of Marriage," 13.

[3]Lonnie Barbach and David L. Geisinger, *Going the Distance: Secrets to Lifelong Love* (New York: Doubleday, 1991), 7–8.

[4]Gleick, "Should This Marriage Be Saved?" 50–51.

[5]Ibid.

[6]Karen S. Peterson, "Breaking Patterns to Hold Couples Together," *USA Today*, 6 February 1992, D6.

[7]Stowell, "The Divorce Dilemma," 15.

[8]Rowell, "Adult Runaways," 70.

[9]Janice Hearn, *Peace with the Restless Me* (Waco: Word, 1976), 104–5.

[10]Ivars Peterson, "Ribbon of Chaos," *Science News* 139 (26 January 1991): 60–61.

Eleven

Jack Fell Down and Jill Came Tumbling After
Faithful to the End

> Great living is like [a great symphony] . . . great convictions which life develops, expands, elevates, and glorifies, fine at the beginning, loveliest of all at the last.[1]

It was the night of my husband's graduation from seminary. In a few short days I'd be a pastor's wife. No big deal, except for the fact we'd just endured several years of intense conflict in our home church. And the church we were about to serve had experienced strife in the past. People clashes always unnerve me. I was very fearful of the future.

My in-laws and I inched our way up the aisle of the large sanctuary crammed with friends and relatives of the graduates. As we edged along the pews, an unusual sight caught our eyes. A few feet away a woman lay stretched flat on her back on a full-size hospital bed.

My mother-in-law reached her first. She gave the woman a warm greeting, then leaned closer to grasp her labored response. "They didn't think I'd make it, but I did!" she whispered. "I just had to be here to see him . . . I just had to!"

The surge of the throng behind us made further talk impossible. Yet, this woman's powerful, living testimony given from the confines of a sickly body wouldn't let me go. Her goal was survival, with a purpose. She endured the humiliation and pain. She'd discarded the excuses. She ignored the pitying stares of passersby. She cared enough about someone else to be there.

Good Housekeeping magazine compiled the names of 100 significant women, from 1885–1985, who were noted for their distinguished contributions. They were nominated by Barnard, Bryn Mawr, Goucher, and Radcliffe colleges.

Each woman named had committed herself to a particular cause, such as Susan B. Anthony; or overcome tremendous difficulty, such as Helen Keller. Each was *devoted* to something or someone.

To what are we committed? To whom are we devoted?

Faithful—that's what we want to be. Faithful to our imperfect marriages. Faithful to our time- and energy-consuming kids. Faithful to our smattering of friendships, our persistent duties, to all we were created to be and purposed to do. Faithful to God. Faithful, to our life's end. Faithful for our sakes, for the sake of those who depend on us, for the sake of the generation to come.

Faithful. What a lofty ideal, a treasured objective. However, today, we may feel like running away. And what will keep us from it?

Those who want to be faithful to something or someone outside themselves are at cross-purposes with our world. We're surrounded by runaways. Our society is diseased by the increasing strains of social ills. We're the product of a culture steeped in runaway behavior and thinking. We're influenced by sheer repetition and the persistent pervasion of its world view.

"If it feels right, it must be okay."

"You deserve to do something for yourself."

"Everybody's doing it."

"Stand up for your rights! Never mind about them." Though we may call ourselves Christian, we're influenced by incessant, daily propaganda to be unfaithful. How do we keep from straying from the constraints of roles and duties when we also want some privileges and an occasional exemption? We're not asking for much, surely. We want liberty, independence, freedom. Isn't that the American way?

When we don't get release, when we feel tied and bound while those around us appear to be free as loose balloons, we get an itch to run. When there's ferment, turmoil, chaos, we long for peace, order, and ease.

What keeps us plowing our own dry, crusty field when the sun's beating down and we're thirsty and we long for cool, green meadows of rest and shade? Just over there, down the driveway, beyond the gate.

Faithful. What a sweet and tender dream.

But is it really that important? After all, what will one more runaway matter? And why is being faithful so much better?

The Rewards

What prize would be worthy of keeping us faithful in the long, cold winter fogs and the incessant traffic jams of life?

"I stay to give God pleasure," a friend tells me.

Faithful in this world, in order to prepare for the next. That keeps some steady while toughing it out.

He who stands firm to the end will be saved.
Matthew 10:22

Be faithful, even to the point of death, and I will give you the crown of life.
Revelation 2:10

Faithfulness deserves recognition and honor and praise. The faithful deserve rewards. Tantalizing promises are made of great rewards in heaven. Jesus was motivated by rewards to persevere through terrible tortures.

> Let us fix our eyes on Jesus, the author and perfecter of our faith, *who for the joy set before him* endured the cross, scorning its shame, and sat down at the right hand of the throne of God.
>
> Hebrews 12:2 (italics added)

The faithful are those with eternity in their souls.

Sometimes faithfulness is its own reward—the steady building of inner character and outer graces, the lack of fallout and damage in relationships.

Faithfulness can provide these rewards: an inheritance to pass on, satisfaction of a job well done, healing to the rejected, family security and continuity, protection and strength, resiliency and hardiness, recognition for higher service.

Children benefit from seeing long-term love in action. They learn to trust.

The Long Haul

Faithfulness. What is it exactly?

Faithfulness is an undivided heart, a person who's completely trustworthy to stand firmly beside us—no matter what. Faithfulness is planned, purposeful kindness, the doing of duties, the keeping of promises. Faithfulness is adjusting to the changing of seasons and transitions, flexing with the flow. Faithfulness depends on what I'm doing and thinking right now.

Faithfulness is a process. It's many daily deeds. It's much working through feelings and doubts and decisions until a line is crossed, a marker is gouged. It's the daily determination to steadily move forward. At some point a certain moment passes and we know ever after a commitment's firm. It's developed by keeping our word, by being where we say we are, by doing what we say we're doing. It's building integrity by proving trust in practical, daily exercises.

Faithfulness means a lot of long, dry days with nothing grandiose in them. Faithfulness is dull at times. But the practice builds us up to a sturdy force that makes possible the doing of great things, courageous things, the suddenly in-your-face things, when they're needed.

What are the traits, the resources, that are a part of being in that number, the march of the faithful?

Devotion

Who, or what, are we fighting *for,* rather than *against?*

At life's end, who will we want with us? Folks who just happen to be there? Or special ones with whom we've gone the distance in growing together, learning together, making constant recommitment together?

Do we have any goals or purposes that are higher than ourselves? Or are they all centered on me, myself, and I. What is important to us—no matter what?

Barbara Bush, wife of the former president, explained her thoughts about life's most significant priorities to a graduating class at Wellesley College. She exhorted the women to "believe in something larger than yourself. Get involved in some of the big ideas of our time," but also to cherish connections with family and friends.[2]

The challenging practice of nourishing relationships helps us overcome our fears of intimacy and rejection. It also is key to learning faithfulness.

Hope

Discouragement cuts the heart and leaves no spirit for the rigors of being faithful. Hope can be tenacious, but most times it's like a flighty bird.

> Hope is the thing with feathers—
> That perches in the soul.[3]

We must avoid impossible goals that leave us hopeless. We've got to believe that we can attain what we desire. We need some basis, rooted in reality and the test of experiences, for believing that faithfulness is worth the trouble it takes, and that it is possible to achieve. That means accomplishing this massive, noble task one hair's breadth at a time.

Hope is most poignant and welcome after long sieges of grief, sorrow, or distress. We struggle to find an answer, a release; then gradually we find an idea, a person, a principle—a spark, a touch, a deliverance—that washes us with welcome comfort of renewed strength. Again, we're on the road to faithfulness. Then, we can share this blessing, this benediction, with others who aren't quite there yet: "May the God of hope fill you with all joy and peace as you trust in him, so that you may overflow with hope by the power of the Holy Spirit" (Romans 15:13).

Contentment

A former runaway relates her present condition. "This is the best time of my life. I'm striving to know God better and learning how to wait on Him. I'm part of a good church fellowship. My husband loves me. I have good friends. However, I do realize I have far to go. . . . It's harder now because once you've run away, you know you can do it. Now I constantly fight the urge to run from any unpleasant circumstance."

Contentment does not mean that everything is perfect, or that we have arrived. Neither should it mean that we're sedated, sedentary, and complacent. It means we're satisfied where we are and doing everything we can to make it right, good, or better.

Contentment is peace in the midst of conflict. It's taking control over anxiety and placing our trust in God. For the Christian, contentment is "that sweet, inward, quiet, gracious frame of spirit, which freely submits to and delights in God's wise and fatherly disposal in every condition."[4]

Contentment notices what has been taken away, but also delights in whatever is left, and looks forward to what might be given in the future. We learn how to live with unfulfillment for "unfulfilled dreams are a fact of life."[5] In fact, fulfilled dreams often make us empty, restless—even depressed. The ideal husband has his difficult side, our beautiful babies grow up to whine and rebel, the perfect career leaves us hungering for something more.

Spiritual contentment is finding home, but ever searching for ways to use it for the benefit of others.

Endurance

Faithfulness requires total commitment to a person or cause or project during good and bad times. To endure the crush of problems. To endure the people. To endure the monotony with no perks, no cooperation, not even thanks.

Faithfulness to be true must be tested. It is established and proven through trials and temptations and failing and getting up to go again. Growing faithful happens during struggle. Life's most meaningful and satisfying experiences often come after much struggle. Struggles require tenacity, creativity, and vital times of reassessment. Struggles save us from self-deception, our fatal blind sides. Struggle makes us more human and God more real.

Striving is the important part because starting power and staying power are not the same. In fact, we can't absolutely be called faithful while we're still living. It's a bit premature. To the grave—that's how long it takes.

A Piece of Courage

When we take time to think things through, sort out the confusion, allow our spirits as well as our minds to grow, we're more confident. When we snuggle down in the richness of God—His incredible promises, His wise commands, His fascinating character—we find resolution of our restlessness. We begin to freely express what we feel, what we believe, what we know to be truth by a standard outside ourselves. We're ready to stand alone if need be, to face our world "in all its perilous and overpowering aspects."[6] We have the boldness to be faithful.

Courage is learning to stand on our own feet, with the full sense of human frailty, but knowing God is behind us.[7]

Courage is a cheerful spirit.

Courage is encouragement stirred by faithful friends.

Courage is believing God will never fail us nor forsake us.

Courage is confidence that God's hand is on us.

Courage is something we do, not something we feel.

Courage is discipline, making difficult decisions, and telling ourselves the truth.

Courage is doing our best in taking on a new challenge, and seeing it through to the end.

Courage is admitting personal sin—no excuses, no blaming others, no toning down.

Courage is doing the work assigned to us when we absolutely don't feel like it.

Courage is confidence that God is good and wants to do us good.

Pamela tried to find courage in a bottle, and bombed out instead. She only dug a deeper crater for herself. "Now, I not only need the courage and grit to get off the sauce-dependence," she admits, "I still have to learn how to cope with the ordinary stuff of living."

She's finding strength in the Bible instead. "I've memorized some verses in Joshua and Psalms that give me a wonderful mental picture of how God's helping me. I do my little part and He brings out His army. Verses like:

> One of you routs a thousand, because the Lord your God fights for you, just as he promised. So be very careful to love the Lord your God.
>
> Joshua 23:10-11

"And I love this one:

> I am still confident of this: I will see the goodness of the Lord in the land of the living.
>
> Psalm 27:3

"The land of the living . . . that means now, on this earth, in this life . . . I feel stronger just saying these words."

A Change of Heart

It's not always the jerks in our lives who keep us from being faithful. Many times we're the problem.

The heart is the seat of the personality, the spring of all our motives and affections. Fickle, erratic behavior originates with the condition of our hearts.[8]

The most dramatic miracle is change in the human heart, when a will is redirected by insight, by divine light, by a wider panorama of what life's all about. When that happens we see a proud heart humbled, an evil heart purged, a grieving heart comforted, a divided heart focused, a foolish heart made wise, a selfish heart elevated, a hardened heart softened, a hateful heart full of affection, a deceitful heart made honest, a straying heart determined to be faithful, a runaway heart longing for home.

"Create in me a pure heart, O God, and renew a steadfast spirit within me" (Psalm 51:10), King David cried out when he despaired that he'd lost sight of God's favor forever.

Cherishing Human Connections

Love that lasts—healthy, lifelong partnerships based on affection and respect—if that isn't a miracle cure for all that ails us it's at least a hearty stopgap.

When we begin to understand one other person outside ourselves, we develop empathy. And empathy pushes us to gather more information, to try harder, to get on the road called Faithful.

> By its very nature, a friendship cannot be nurtured on the run.[9]

Family is a permanent connection. We had no choice. We're stuck with where we were planted. But most friends are chosen—because of where we live, or how they make us laugh, or because we share values or interests.

But family can become friends, and friends can become like family. That crossover usually happens when we're superstressed, overwrought and life hands us a blow that threatens to scatter those near and far. Some stay, and we practice faithfulness on each other.

Rizpah remained faithful, even after the dishonorable death of her two sons and five of her husband's grandsons. She stood guard over their exposed bodies for five months—from barley harvest until fall rain. They had been killed because they belonged to Saul's family, a king considered responsible for a severe famine because of his disobedience to God.

Rizpah drove away the wild animals and vultures. She endured the stifling heat of day, and the bitter nights. She endured the stares of pity. She endured the chants of derision. Silent, alone, she poignantly typifies a mother who cherished her family connections. When King David hears of her vigil, he commands that the family of Saul's concubine receive an honorable burial (2 Samuel 21:1–14).

Covenants

Commitment is scary. It provides security, but also loss of control, loss of choices, loss of freedoms. It can make us full of fear: can we keep our part of the bargain? And can they, will they—that is, the other partner—keep theirs?

A covenant is a commitment that's usually a written agreement under seal between two parties. Each makes a solemn pledge of faithfulness to certain acts and to each other.

Covenants were the earliest law to be found in the Bible. The first was made by God with the people of Israel after their escape from Egypt: "You will be my people, and I will be your God." The Ten Commandments were the core of this covenant and highlighted the importance of love for God and love for neighbors (see Exodus 19–20; Leviticus 26:12; Jeremiah 11:4; 30:22).

Covenants with God are made possible through Jesus Christ. The example of His life, His death on our behalf, the strength His Spirit gives now provides a motivation and means to keep our part of the relationship with God. We desperately need this assistance of a method of forgiveness and starting over, of obtaining new birth and new hearts.[10]

A covenant relationship is a promise given. When God is included, we call upon Him to help accomplish the covenant, to supply what human resources cannot. A covenant relationship is a potentially forever bond, such as between a ruler and the people he rules, between a man and woman in marriage. It's a pledge of belonging and serving. Jonathan and David made a covenant like this. So did Ruth with her mother-in-law, Naomi (see 1 Samuel 20:16–17; Ruth 1:16–17).

A covenant requires action, not just mental assent, and it is needed when a promise of loyalty is essential to the carrying out of a particular relationship or partnership. This thing can't be done alone; it requires two. And it must be done by these specific persons. No one else can do it in quite the same way, with the same satisfying results. It's the kind of bond made by people who are "willing to fulfill the other's need without regard for repayment or public recognition or personal convenience."[11]

A covenant is a pledge, a contract that establishes a close bond, both personal and permanent. It binds people together to pressure them to work through their problems rather than run from them.

It's easier to fall in love than it is to become attached. Attachment is hard work. Much time, energy, and constant effort are necessary to get to know those with whom we make commitments and to live with the commitments we make. Promises can pull us through when anger and despair and disappointment threaten to pull us out.

A covenant exerts some force to communicate with our covenant partners. We can't shut them out when we feel misunderstood or not loved the way we think we should be. A covenant is experiencing a promise at the life-changing level. In marriage it also means "exchanging identities"—taking on, taking up, protecting, defending this one imperfect fellow human with whom we are now connected, bonded, and identified.[12]

A covenant must be entered into carefully, with much thought. We must be fully convinced that this should be and can be done.

There are covenants of love between two people who want to assure each other that they will be cherished and cared for, whatever life brings.

There are covenants of peace. These include specific services to be performed, such as property traded or sold, or boundaries established. This is the reason for the Mizpah covenant between Jacob and his father-in-law, Laban: "May the Lord keep watch between you and me when we are away from each other" (Genesis 31:49; see verses 48–50). Peace was forged in the midst of an atmosphere of distrust and suspicion.

Covenants can be violated or annulled. They can be promises of blessing, with a condition of obedience. Sometimes they include warnings. Some are used to issue a curse. They can be renewed. They can be sealed with a sign, such as Jacob's memorial stones, or a symbol, such as God's rainbow in the sky (see Genesis 9:12–16; 28:18–22).

Commitments are voluntary. The word, even the contract, can be broken. Emotions come and go. Promises and obligations and honor are only as important as the character and desires within a very secret and malleable part of the human heart. But covenants can steady the soul and make it so much harder to be unfaithful.

Staying Power

In front of me is a magazine with the pictures and stories of two women to whom they are paying tribute. They're praised for their "shining faith, compassion, and courage," for their commitments that have "touched and [are] still touching thousands of lives with profound inspiration and blessing."[13]

Corrie ten Boom

She lived the first fifty years of her life in relative obscurity as a watchmaker in her father's shop in Haarlem, Holland. During World War II she and her family harbored Jews from the Nazis. This led to the arrest and imprisonment of the ten Boom family, in which they endured the atrocities of the concentration camps.

When Corrie was released, she began telling the world how God had encouraged her and her sister, Betsy, in the black suffering of horrendous conditions, the many lessons they learned. When Corrie died in 1983 at the age of ninety-one, she had traveled to more than sixty countries and authored eighteen books. Faithful in the mundane details of family life, faithful in the darkest pits of despair, this woman speaks power to folks like us.

Catherine Marshall

The author of eighteen books, she persisted in her faith through bouts of tuberculosis, widowhood, single parenting, remarriage, and the trials of stepmothering. Each stage of her life's pilgrimage was difficult and demanding, but she didn't run.

When several grandchildren died after copious prayer on their behalf, she asked God, "Why?" but she didn't run.

In March, 1983, Catherine's last challenge ended. She was faithful to the grave. She earned respect and admiration due a role model and teacher from those of us still struggling, still wondering, still hoping to reach the finish line, unashamed.

Faithful.

That's who we think we are. Most of the time. Until we get into tight spots, conflicts, fierce temptation, persecution. Until we face troubling doubts or debilitating fears or feelings of desperation.

Sometimes we feel so alone. It's hard to be faithful in isolation. We need the support and example of role models.

It seems as though even the saints are blowing it, that no one stands true, that no one cares enough to stick it out.

Elijah felt that way too. A great man of God with an impressive, forceful beginning, he trembled in hiding in a cave. He was afraid, so he ran. God met him where he was, huddled in his dark hole, and told him he wasn't alone. There were others, at least seven thousand others, who were faithful in trials, who didn't run (see 1 Kings 19).

Surely there are many more than that today.

We could be there in that number. But we won't be if we skip out, chuck it all, cave in, go over the hill. However, we can be if we learn how to ease the steam off the boiler, find our steady pace, keep on track, find the breaks that keep us from running.

But what's in it for us? Why be faithful? So we'll hear the most precious words ever uttered to any human:

"Well done, good and faithful servant! You have been faithful with a few things; I will put you in charge of many things. Come and share your master's happiness!" (Matthew 25:21).

Discovery Questions

1. Who is the most spiritual woman you know?
    Why do you think this about her?

2. Read the story of Elijah in 1 Kings 18 and 19. How do you explain Elijah's rapid fall from courage and boldness to running for his life?

    Have you ever experienced a sudden shift in faith or bravado such as this? When and why?

3. Have you ever been part of a covenant relationship? Explain.
    What are the positive and negative aspects?
    Is there someone now you would like to join in such a bond, and why?

4. Below are sample definitions of *faithfulness*. Which do you object to, and why? Which is most meaningful to you, and why?
    a. Prompt, active, and efficient promotion of the interests of another
    b. Diligence in developing the capacity for doing or becoming something
    c. Eagerness for higher service
    d. Making the most of what little you have
    e. Trusting God's power and love in danger, struggle, and sorrow
    f. Constant obligation
    g. Dependency upon and responsibility toward someone else

h. Cheerful and unreserved dedication
i. Enduring imperfection

5. Which of the following best describes *un*faithfulness, and why?
    a. Setting before yourself a low or unworthy ideal
    b. Allowing timidity or laziness to extinguish all enthusiasm
    c. Doing nothing at all
    d. Neglecting the aid of God's grace
    e. Unprofitable service
    f. Refusal to bring blessing to a fellow human
    g. Disobedience to a merciful heavenly parent
    h. Dishonoring a reputation
    i. Running away

6. Read Matthew 25:14–30. What impresses you most about this parable?
    If you personally heard these words from Jesus—"Well done!"—what would be your first reaction? Surprise? Humility? Worship? Love?
    How much would these words be worth to you?

7. Can a runaway ever become loyal and faithful and reap the rewards?
    What are some of the problems? The blessings?

8. Write down at least three comments you have to make about this statement: We don't know if we're truly faithful until we've been tested.

9. Read 1 Corinthians 4:1–5. What does this have to say about faithfulness?

10. Read Job 31:1.

What do you think about Job's covenant? Is it a good one?

An effective one? Why?

If you were making a promise to yourself today, what would it be?

11. Read Acts 28:15–16.

What encouraged Paul to endure his distresses?

12. Optional Bonus Exercise: Read Nehemiah 8:1–10:39. This describes the *renewing* of a covenant between God and the Jewish people.

What was God's part? What was the people's part?

Why did the covenant have to be renewed?

What importance did this covenant have in the lives of the people?

What kind of relationship do you think God was striving for by initiating such a covenant?

Notes

[1]Harry Emerson Fosdick, "The Power to See It Through," *Twenty Centuries of Great Preaching*, vol. 9, ed. Clyde E. Fant, Jr. and William M. Pinson, Jr. (Waco: Word, 1971), 55.

[2]Rolf Zettersten, "Words Worth Remembering," *Focus on the Family*, August 1990, 23.

[3]Emily Dickinson, in *Familiar Quotations* by John Bartlett (Boston: Little, Brown, 1980), 604:17.

[4]J. Burroughs, *The Rare Jewel of Christian Contentment* (Newark, Del.: Cornerstone), 2.

[5]Donald McCullough, "The Pitfalls of Positive Thinking," *Christianity Today*, 6 September 1985, 23.

[6]Fromm, *Escape from Freedom*, 29.

[7]Charles C. Ryrie, *The Ryrie Study Bible*, New International Version, notes on Philippians 2:12–18 (Chicago: Moody, 1986), 1625.

[8]Gerald B. Griffiths, "The Secret of Steady Perseverance," *Decision*, June 1990, 26.

[9]Fish, "Caught between Expectations," 15.

[10]Keeley, *Eerdmans' Handbook to Christian Belief*, 243–44, 465.

[11]Katherine Doob Sakenfeld, "Loyalty and Love: The Language of Human Interconnections in the Hebrew Bible," *Michigan Quarterly Review*, 203.

[12]J. Thompson and P. Thompson, *Dance of the Broken Heart*, 147–49, 177.

[13]"Corrie ten Boom and Catherine Marshall," *Virtue*, September/October 1983, 6.

Twelve

The Other Side of Old Faithful

Goldie and Myra are sisters, seven years apart. The eldest, Goldie, tells her pilgrimage in her relationship with Myra.

"As a teen, I felt that Myra dishonored our parents with her greedy, selfish, and immoral ways. But she finally seemed to get herself together. She got a job as the director of a large preschool facility and everyone I talked to said she got along great with the kids and the staff and even the parents. Then, one day, she ran off. I was shocked, ashamed, and angry. She was gone without explanation for over a year. We never really knew where she was or why.

"Then, as suddenly as she disappeared, she came back. My mom was a little cautious at first, but she soon welcomed Myra with open arms. My dad was ecstatic. Myra seemed happier than ever. As for me, the whole affair was troublesome. I didn't want to talk to her, to see her or think about her. She was still gone, as far as I was concerned. Somehow, she deserved punishment, at least some estrangement. My secret prayer was, 'Lord, surely she should suffer a little. It was all too quick, too smooth.' But the topper came when she got her old job back. I had my doubts whether Myra would ever walk the straight and narrow. Surely, she still didn't know how to be dependable.

"I stewed about this for a long time, and Myra knew it. Then, one day in church, the preacher let me have it. 'Have you any right to be angry?' he said over and over, quoting out of the book of Jonah. I sat straight up. It was as though God had taken hold of this man's mind and mouth and was talking right to me.

"Jonah had been a runaway. But God chased him down until he agreed to preach to despicable sinners and get them saved! How dare they! Jonah pouted and fussed about it plenty. It hit me! I was Jonah—*both* as a runaway and as a whiner on the side. I was running away from my God-given privilege to shout 'hallelujah' with the angels every time the lost came home. In addition, I felt God point out every private sin I tried so hard to tuck away—from myself, as well as from others. My sister's sin, He seemed to be telling me, just happened to be public.

"As soon as I left the church, I raced to my sister's house. I couldn't get there fast enough. I told her I had a change of heart and why. She cried her heart out. We talked for hours as she told me how she felt she could never be as good as me, that she could never measure up, and how panicked she'd been when her job overwhelmed her. She thought she might be fired, and she couldn't bear seeing her folks disappointed again. For the first time in our lives, we're really close."

Forgiveness is hard. It's hard because we're self-centered; we can see only our side, our hurt, the offense done to our pride or dreams. We're governed by our emotions and don't want to let go of the resentment.

Forgiveness is very hard. Because we're unloving, love has to be learned. True love has to be willed, practiced; but it still requires a divine spark to soften the stubborn hardness in us all. The matter hits too close to the heart, and our heart's not at peace, and we don't always understand why.

Forgiveness is almost impossible because the offense often takes something important away from us; because forgiving doesn't always fix things or change the offender quickly; because the problems still require attention, we still suffer our loss; because we're afraid or mistrusting of the offender and what she may do next. And the bitterness, anger, fear, or mistrust can rob us of "the vision of restoration."[1]

Forgiveness can rankle the faithful.

Job's wife never ran away. She was faithful, in her fashion. She was also cranky, insensitive, and completely frustrated. "Curse God and die," she advised her husband (see Job 2:7–10).

Faithful does not necessarily mean perfect.

There are two sides to this ideal we call faithful. Sometimes we look like we're persevering under intense opposition when we're really the opposition. Only our hearts know for sure.

The Elder Sister

When someone runs away, she usually leaves behind an "elder sister." The elder sister can be a friend, a relative, a coworker, or an acquaintance. As the dust clears from the run, the elder sister assesses the responses of feelings of those around her—to the one who absconded, and to herself. The intensity of her own emotions about the situation, as well as desires and needs in her own circumstance, come to the fore.

The "younger" has flitted off to "a distant country"— for adventures, to squander her days and resources. She's in rebellion, in sin. The elder sister is full to the gills with righteous indignation.

Then, as the elder sister sees it, when the younger is no longer able to care for herself, or isn't properly prepared for unforeseen emergencies, or is hungry enough or lonely enough, she comes home. "She'll do anything to come back, even ask forgiveness," she thinks. "Watch her grovel in front of them all. She's getting all the attention. I've been here holding everything together. But I'm ignored. I'm the fixture, the familiar object, the one to be taken for granted. It's not fair! It's not right!"

Or the runaway may find a better place and want to stay there. Either way, the elder sister is left to fume. She's faithful. She works hard at her appointed rounds. But it's expected, not appreciated. For years she slaves. She never rebels. But she gets no respect; that is, not in the way she wants it. She is faithful, but not content.

The elder sister's inner turmoil prompts a reassessment. Is she truly "home"? Is she where she wants to be? Why is she faithful—because of love? Because of duty? Because she's healthy, prosperous, and pampered? Because she has no choice? Why is she so upset with the one who ran? Because of the damage done to innocents? Or because of jockeying for position? Because she detests nasty surprises, people who can't be counted on? Because she's a perfectionist who has to earn love? Uncomfortable questions like these will help the elder sister work through her motives.

While the runaway was running, the elder sister could play the part of the steady, faithful one, the one deserving of praise, the one who would comfort the hurting, give advice, be there. The repentant, returning runaway not only grates on her righteous sensibilities, but also changes her status. While outwardly she may make concessions, inwardly she seethes with the discomfort of sharing the stage with this unworthy one. Who will need her now? How will her long-standing, faithful demeanor shine above this upstart's efforts at being a regular person?

The lost one is found, and the elder sister doesn't much like it. The runaway is finally hit by the hard knocks of reality, something the elder sister had hold of all along.

Elder sisters need compassion, affirmation, loving attention, and understanding. The problem is, they're usually harder to love, more difficult to care about, testier to compliment because of their prickly, though faithful, attitudes.

The elder sister has a point. She can make her case, for what the individual does has repercussions on the whole community. We need elder sisters. They bring balance and steadiness and keep things sane when we're prone to hysteria.

But the glory for the elder sister comes when she works through her virtuous wrath and comes to stand by the one to whom she could say, "I told you so," and tells her instead, "I care; how are you doing?" Both sisters have a need to come to the Father heart of God and find His instruction and blessing.

Those who suffer are pitied. Those freed from suffering are celebrated. Those who walk away from suffering are reviled by the faithful.

The Paradox of Loyalty

When executives of a major airline decided to downsize, they summoned several hundred employees—many of whom had been with the company twenty years or more—to an auditorium. The door was closed by a security guard who then stood in front of it. A company representative strode to the podium and somberly announced, "We regret to inform you that as of today you are no longer employed. You will be escorted to your work area by a guard to pick up your personal effects."

The employees were shocked and angry. Most had no idea of what was coming. Most had given long years of loyal service and never received so much as a "thank you."[2]

Those who are faithful expect a measure of security. But they don't always get it. Life is unfair sometimes.

We can be loyal, yet the object of our loyalty mistrusts us, can betray us, or can become an outright enemy. Our desire to serve and commit to another may not be reciprocated. This can lead to emotional injury, and an unwillingness to trust again.

On the other hand, loyalty must be freely chosen in order to be sincere and complete. Conformity, passive submission, and complacency are not the same as loyalty. Loyalty is an active act of the will that has stood the test of time and trials.

Sometimes being loyal to one person or group means being disloyal to another. We have to take sides. A line is drawn and we cross over. At the same time, if we try to see every side of every situation, we don't take any side at all.

Those who are loyal can be taken advantage of, or taken for granted.

Loyalty means choices—loyalty to God, or to country? Loyalty to beliefs, or to family? Loyalty to friends, or to cause? Loyalty to career, or to marriage?

We can be loyal because we recognize that's a value, a good thing. We can be loyal because we feel a duty to those whom we owe a debt. We can be loyal because we're submissive to authority, no matter what happens, and we conform to certain routines, no matter who doesn't fit. We can be loyal to those with whom we have strong bonds—family, friends, coworkers. Or we can be loyal because we're dedicated to a particular individual's welfare.

But our loyalty may be construed as favoritism or bias. And we want to be fair to everyone, or liked by everyone. It's complicated at times to be faithful.

When the Faithful Falter

We're ruled by our moods, our desires, our influences.

We're also prone to be undone in unpleasant circumstances that hang on too long. We can no longer think clearly. We say and do things we wish we hadn't.

When we're disconnected from God, we're adrift in the sea of our blind choices. Spiritual discernment is vital if we're to unravel the half-truths and rationales we tell ourselves.

> The miserable ruin into which the revolt of the first man has plunged us, compels us to turn our eyes upwards . . . for there exists in man something like a world of misery, ever since we were stripped of the divine attire.[3]

When we lack understanding—about our situation or about God's purpose, provision, and power—we tend to harden our hearts. We become bitter or defiant or overcome by hopelessness. These feelings, born out of a darkened mind, are the roots of antisocial and irreligious behavior. They're the seeds in the heart of a potential runaway.

Bitterness is resentment over a perceived or real injustice. If allowed to, it festers until it develops into deep rancor or hostility toward God and an ever-widening circle of people.

Defiance is willful rebellion against rules or laws or expectations. It's contempt for the wishes of another. It's the assertion that we don't need anyone other than ourselves. The defiant person resists any kind of reproof or correction.

Hopelessness is "the feeling that there is no way out, that things will only get worse, and that one is completely helpless."[4]

Can we stay faithful, and bitter?

Can we stay faithful, and defiant?

Can we stay faithful, and feel so hopeless?

"Why do you talk to me that way?" Karen finally got the nerve to ask her husband after years of put-downs and sarcasm. He stared at her, his eyes blank pools of ignorance. "What way?" he finally muttered, rubbing his beer can against his two day growth of whiskers.

That's when she first believed it was useless to try. What she needed and what he would or could give her were worlds apart. She began to build a life of her own—business ventures, committee meetings, friends he didn't know. His harangues dropped soundless into a bottomless pool. She couldn't hear him anymore.

"This is much different than my old way of responding," Karen adds. "I used to be like a turtle, pulling emotionally into my shell. It hurt out there, so I didn't want to be there. I guess both responses are a kind of running away. But, at least I'm still there for him."

God and His Runaway Kids

In our personal lives we're torn by strife, by disappointment, and by distrust. Then, we face heightened stress levels from outside, distorted by life lessons from the instant media that pours the world's evils in concentrated levels into our living rooms. Terrorists' bombs, hate groups, drive-by shootings, political turmoil—we long for comfort and protection for ourselves and our loved ones. Our reason is garbled by the force of terror and hysteria. We're tied in knots trying to control our lives and circumstances. Cynicism reigns.[5]

> Turn to me and be gracious to me,
> for I am lonely and afflicted.
>
> Psalm 25:16

We're at our wit's end, total despair. It seems as though it's all over. We're helpless and hopeless, vulnerable to a storm that's been unleashed against and around us. We're fainting with fear, paralyzed by frustration, powerless to do anything but run.

> The troubles of my heart have multiplied;
> free me from my anguish.
>
> Psalm 25:17

We're restless inside. There's a dull pain in the heart, a sinking sureness that nothing will change, that the persistent agony is permanent. We're in a desolate, lonely place.

> Look upon my affliction and my distress
> and take away all my sins.
> See how my enemies have increased
> and how fiercely they hate me!
>
> Psalm 25:18–19

Everyone seems against us. There's no one to help, no one to listen. That's our heart, the heart of a runaway. We want to cry out, like the psalmist, "Why, O Lord, do you stand far off? Why do you hide yourself in times of trouble?" (Psalm 10:1).

But God sees our heart. And what does He do?

He comes to where we are. He meets us at the end of the run. He knows where to find us. He knows the whole situation. He usually asks probing questions. He wants to get at what's deep inside us—the real reason we're running—not just the rationales we spring on other people or the half-truths we rehearse over and over to ourselves; not only our thoughts, but our intentions, the trigger motives. This may take some time. He's in no hurry. He's had a lot of experience with runaways.

Adam and Eve—the original runners. Ashamed to face God, they hid behind trees. But God finds them, calls out to them, questions them, and metes out His fatherly discipline: they lost their home in Paradise (see Genesis 3).

Hagar—a forced concubine, an insolent servant. She is mistreated by Sarah, her mistress, so she runs away. God sends an angel to find her, near a spring in the desert. "Where have you come from, and where are you going?" he asks. Then, the angel encourages her to return home after giving her promises and prophecies about the baby in her womb (see Genesis 16).

Jacob—ran in fear from his brother, Esau, whom he cheated out of his birthright. God meets him in a dream and gives him promises. Years later, Jacob runs again, this time from his father-in-law, Laban, and back toward his brother. The angels of God meet him on the way. One of them wrestles with him, injuring his hip socket, then blesses him (see Genesis 32–33).

Moses—at the age of forty, seeks to bring about a good thing (deliverance of his people) in a wrong way (via murder). He has to run for his life. The next four decades in exile are a kind of penitence and training ground as he tends sheep in the Midian wilderness—until one day God calls to him from a burning bush to return home (see Exodus 2:11–16; 3).

Saul—ran and hid when God tried to choose him to be the first king of Israel. God knew right where he was. "In the baggage," He told Samuel and the people. God had to change Saul's heart and empower him with His Spirit to nudge him out of his shyness before he could begin to be king (see 1 Samuel 10:9, 20–27; 11:6).

Elijah—terrified of Jezebel's threats, he ran. Finally, slumped under a juniper tree, he moaned, "I've had enough! I can't take any more. I want to die!" God sent him his own private angel to be a butler and cook. God said, "Eat and rest." God understood he was hurting, confused, fearful, and full of doubts and questions. He felt useless, at a deadend. God encouraged and exhorted his weary, discouraged servant in a still, small voice (see 1 Kings 19).

Jonah—when he ran from God, the Lord chased after him with a violent storm at sea and a great fish to swallow him and vomit him up on dry land. When he finally did what he was told—preach a warning to the people of Nineveh—he pouted about God's kindness to them. God took time to meet him on his dump heap of self-pity and reason with him (see Jonah 1, 4).

Onesimus—wanted freedom from slavery, so he stole from his master, Philemon, and ran. God brought him to Christ through the apostle Paul, who also interceded for him to his master through a letter which comprises the whole book of Philemon.

> [God] tends His flock like a shepherd.
> He gathers the lambs in his arms
> and carries them close to his heart;
> he gently leads those that have young.
> Isaiah 40:11

If one of them wanders away, or runs off, He goes after them (Luke 22:31). He understands their journey and travels it with them.

God is most precious in our most difficult times because we see Him in the role of heavenly Father. He wants our childlike trust and confidence in Him. He wants to hear us say: "It is tough and crazy right now, but my Father knows the way. He has a plan. Meanwhile, what shall I give Him? I'll give Him my heart."

He always comes to us as a Father—with a helping hand, an offer of love and guidance, always with a listening ear—even when He comes to discipline us. As long as there is life, there is hope. As long as time is ticking away, Father and daughter can be reunited.

> He never, ever abandons us. If we are faithless, he will remain faithful, for he cannot disown himself.
>
> 2 Timothy 2:13

His love pursues us even when we hide our faces from Him, when we run from God-appointed situations. Some of the most moving and revealing pictures of God through the Bible come when He deals with runaways.

"Simon, Simon," Jesus calls out to the disciple who denied him, "Satan has asked to sift you as wheat. But I have prayed for you, Simon, that your faith may not fail. And when you have turned back, strengthen your brothers" (Luke 22:31).

We try so hard to conceal ourselves in dark corners, at the back of the crowd, in the shadows of a hidden cave—to be free of hassle, to be safe. But no matter where we go in all the universe, God knows where we are.

We try to hide from God with hectic, busy lifestyles; behind intellectual baggage; by staying biblically ignorant; in the smoke screen of the needs of others; in the bushes of spiritual isolation. We hide in our comfort zones. We steal away into our prejudiced centers or our base of perceptions. We're all runaways, and He wants us back.

God comes to us where we are in order to put some fight back into us, to teach us how to stand rather than to run away. He wants us out of hiding to face our demons, our common enemies, to face fear with faith.

We can try with everything we've got to be faithful, and not get the results we expected.

We can be faithful, and the runaway gets the spotlight.

We can be faithful for a long time and peak out at the last, undone by the pressures within and without.

That's when Satan delights in convincing us that we're no use to anyone, especially God. But God delights in building cathedrals out of our rubble.[6]

Whether we're faithful or run away, elder or younger sister, found at home or in a cave, we're all potential trophies of His grace.

Discovery Questions

1. Read Luke 15:11–32.
    Have you ever been put in a position like the older brother?
    If so, what was the hardest thing to endure?

2. Read 2 Timothy 4:9–16.
    Have you ever had a similar experience? Explain.

    Read 2 Timothy 4:17–18.
    What was Paul's conclusion?
    What was yours?

3. What do these verses say about being faithful or loyal?

    Joshua 24:15—

    Psalm 37:34—

    Hosea 6:1–3—

    Matthew 24:45–51—

    Luke 9:57–62—

Luke 16:1–13—

Philippians 3:12–14—

Hebrews 2:1–4—

Hebrews 12:1–3—

4. When are the times we *should* run?

5. Read Genesis 32.
    What were the steps Jacob took to reconcile with his brother, Esau?

Notes

[1]Bogle, letter.

[2]Sala, "If Loyalty Is Out, Then What's In?" *Guidelines for Living*, May 1995, 3.

[3]James M. Houston, "The Independence Myth," *Christianity Today*, 15 January 1990, 32.

[4]Armand Mayo Nicholi II, "Why Can't I Deal with Depression?" *Christianity Today*, 11 November 1983, 40.

[5]Dollee Meredith, "If You Give In to God, You Won't Cave In to Sin," *Christian News*, 1–15 May 1995, 8.

[6]January 18, *The Daily Walk*, ed. Bruce H. Wilkinson, January 1995.

Thirteen

Do We Know Where Our Home Is?

Our son Aaron, when four years old, was asked where his home was. He answered, "I live in Fillmore, California, but I was raised in Idaho." Though he'd lived in Idaho for only fifteen months, that seemed like his whole life. He remembered it as home.

Where or what is home? How do we find it?

Home is a place, a person or people, or a philosophy which, in part or whole, completes who we are. It is our base from which we relate to and interpret the events of our world.

Home can be so sure a place that we rattle off its description without hesitation. For others, it may be discovered only after a lifelong process of searching. When we don't know where home is, so much of our energies are spent in searching for it. Some want a home, but never find it. Some want to be home, but aren't allowed there. Some know exactly where home is, but run from it. Some find home and settle in.

Bharati Mukherjee, born in India, spent her life searching for a home. She found it in America. "I knew the moment I landed . . . this is where I belonged. It was an instant kind of love, a feeling of being at one. You see for me, America is an idea. It is a stage for transformation. I felt . . . that suddenly I could be a new person. . . . Home is a state of mind."[1]

Home Sweet Home

It's harder than ever to find a home today.

For one thing, fewer literal four-wall dwellings are being built. The ones that exist are unaffordable for a growing number of our population. Housing is a game of musical chairs. Thousands of families are left out.

Based on a twenty-nine-city survey, the U.S. Conference of Mayors reported in 1987 that families comprise 34 percent of the overall homeless population. And 70 percent to 90 percent of homeless families are headed by women. The remaining families are headed by couples who generally become homeless after the man has lost his job.[2]

Saint Paul knew what it was like: "To this very hour we go hungry and thirsty, we are in rags, we are brutally treated, we are homeless. We work hard with our own hands. When we are cursed, we bless; when we are persecuted, we endure it; when we are slandered, we answer kindly. Up to this moment we have become the scum of the earth, the refuse of the world" (1 Corinthians 4:11–13).

Increasing hordes of the homeless are crammed in shelters, stuffed in cars and camper shells, sprawled over our streets and vacant lots and parks and campgrounds and forests, and even cornered in laundromats.

A woman and her fifteen-year-old son sneak—late at night—into a local laundromat and leave at dawn. She's looking for a job, "but it's hard without a car and without an address and phone number to give potential employers."

She left Las Vegas earlier in the year "because my son had gotten into trouble there and I wanted him out of that environment." The man she traveled with is gone. She kicked him out when he attempted to hit the boy.[3]

An increasing number of the homeless are families who tumble from one reversal of fortunes to another still worse. Lacking a means of providing for themselves, they become a family on wheels.

Tom and Terri drive a rusty, green station wagon, minus muffler, with bald tires. Now it's home for them and their three smudge-faced toddlers. They're always searching for factory work, always out of gas, always short on food.[4]

Reaching out to the chronic homeless (homeless for longer than a year with no prospects in sight) takes understanding, patience, and a certain toughness. We want homeless people to be compliant, grateful, and mannerly. When your social compass has been obliterated, when you've been on survival mode for so long, it's hard to be sociable in all the Amy Vanderbilt ways. You're disoriented. You're like a wounded dog, liable to bite the hand that tries to feed you. You forget how to belong, how to relate to the community. You can't even be combed and clean. Many develop a handout posture, with a chip on the shoulder: a mixture of pride and defeat.

Becoming homeless usually happens through a series of events, one setback leads to another, starting a cycle of destitution. But its full impact is sudden and far-reaching. It's very difficult to master even the basics of daily living and developing as a human without a home. Without a stable base, we disintegrate. Loss of dignity. At the mercy of strangers. No security against the elements and crime. No peaceful base for parenting. Shame for the kids. Isolated, alone. No outlet for stress. No address. No distinct, respectful identity. No connections. No place to keep our stuff. No privacy. No place to rest and sleep and wash, or even to do the simple act of changing clothes. The self-sufficiency that is expected of any adult is gone. And it can happen to most anyone, at any age.[5]

An eighty-five-year-old woman lost her home when the property her trailer occupied for thirty years was sold out from under her for commercial development. The woman's trailer was too old to meet the new code requirements for relocation to a new lot. But she can't afford any other housing either. With no family and a meager fixed income, at her age she never expected to have to move. The last time I heard she was bunking in the living room with some friends, "only temporarily," until she could figure out what to do.

Having a house to live in is only the first step. Learning to live with the people inside that house is another step. Depending on how long the homeless situation has lasted, relearning social roles and reestablishing respect in the community is a barrier to overcome.

Escalating rental markets, evictions, layoffs and factory shutdowns, single- and two-parent families on limited incomes—even with full-time jobs, domestic chaos, decline in low-income housing, personal misfortunes—theft, illness, fire—that wipe out marginal resources; all of these factors create America's new homeless.[6]

For those who live in economic good times, the plight of the homeless is hard to envision. For people who want things *now*, problems like hunger and homelessness are so frustrating because they're overwhelming and not easily fixed.[7]

We can think of solutions to this problem, but most of them are temporary. Doubling up with friends or family, lodging in a motel room, public shelters, experimental car camps, soup kitchens and pantries, clothing distribution, handouts. They need more than emergency Band-aids; they need resources to help them become independent, ways to find a home of their own.

A homeless family of four, in our own small community, lived two weeks in a tent at our state park campground, then alternated two weeks at another camping site down the mountain and along the Snake River. That was because of the rules limiting the time for any one stay. The father owned a business, but the family couldn't find a rental. So few were available. Those they did get a jump on required first and last month's rent plus a cleaning and damage deposit, much more money than they had at one time. They lived like that for six months, until a church became aware of their problem and helped them financially to get into a place, just as the nights were dipping to below-freezing temperatures.

The homeless can't be lumped into one category and disposed of easily. Each homeless person, each homeless family, is homeless in their own way. Some of the homeless are runaways. And each runaway flees for her own reasons and plops down in her own conditions. But most all need a way to find and maintain home.

Elaine Nelson Thompson tells about her "foster homes."

"While I was sorting out where my real home was, and what I should do next, Lynn and Geoffrey took me into their home, complete with five teenagers, two dogs, assorted cats, and one iguana. The important things they did for me were to provide protection and shelter and, most of all, encourage me to reach out to my own kids, even when times were tense. They loved my kids as much as I did.

"Later I was hired to help care for an elderly couple. But our relationship became closer than employee/employer. They made me part of their family, especially during holidays, the hardest time for me. I could see in both these situations how a family, a home, was supposed to be . . . how people could treat each other and that I was a person who could be loved and cherished."

Jesus didn't go around blaming and analyzing the poor and needy. He healed and helped them.

Finding a Place Called Home

Some houses, some cities feel like home right from the start. Others never do.

Pioneers become homeless for a while as they try to forge a new home. Dissatisfied with the one they left behind, they are "greedy with dreams . . . reckless with hope." They develop the souls of immigrants, hungry for new meanings, full of energy and curiosity to make new lives for themselves. To outsiders their existence may seem "raw, raucous, and messy," rather than the "neat, miniaturized, suburban lives" that we're used to and consider normal.[8]

Abraham was a pioneer. From Ur of the Chaldeans to Haran, down across the desert, into the Jordan Valley, south of the Dead Sea, up into the mountains, through the Negev into Egypt, back to Canaan; Abraham went and Sarah followed. He kept looking for the home God promised him (see Genesis 12:1–4; Hebrews 11:9).

Where do we feel most at home? The answer is different for everyone. For Martha, it was in a kitchen. For Mary, it was at the feet of Jesus. The problem came when Martha demanded more of herself and the situation than she could handle and then blamed Mary for running away from her (Luke 10:38–42).

Finding home can be as simple as starting where we are. What commitments have we already made? How can we make a home out of our present dwelling? With the one who's already beside us?

Sometimes we don't know where home is until we've left it. We look behind us and it shines brighter than any spot we've ever been.

But we certainly can't find something when we don't know what we're looking for.

I Feel It in My Bones

Home can be a town or in someone's arms. It can be a work to create or a family farm. It can be an emotional healing or a log cabin in the woods. Home can be a dream to fulfill or a place we pull off our socks. It's where we're comfortable because we know we're supposed to be here; it's our spot to do the tasks we were purposed to do.

But we can have more than one home.

Home can be a stomping ground, where we spend the most time, the place with which people associate us. It can be where Dad is, or Mom is, or where grandparents live—a place we leave when we're grown up and/or called to higher service, a place to go back to that symbolizes the important events and stages of our growing up years.

Home can be wherever we live with our man in a covenant commitment, where we raise a family, a nesting place, a place to manage and care for. This place is more than a house. It's a peopled place that gives us reasons to care beyond ourselves—people to live for, people to fight for, people to die for.

Home can be where we feel most useful, where we work at tasks that are satisfying to us, where we "exercise creativity and make changes that reflect something of our ideas, experiments, and personality."[9]

Home can be where we feel most comfortable, where we long to be, where we think of most of the time. Home is where basic needs are met, a place where we belong, a place where we're content to stay. Home is not a place where we keep our bags packed, ever looking for greener pastures. Home is a place from which we don't stray.

Home is a place that, once found, liberates our energies to be invested outward. Our base of support and security and consolation has been found.

Home may be a place or a relationship we need to fight to regain, a position that needs rebuilding, a thing lost that must be found. Home is our castle, our treasure.

However, no earthly home is Paradise. The gate is shut and locked to that perfect garden.

Tending the Hearth

Home is not always an easy place, a spot without struggle.

Home cannot fill every expectation we have, every moment of every day. That's heaven. We're not there, yet. Home can be a trying place, a difficult person. It's normal to find pressure and battles in a place called home.

We can make mistakes in our home, and so can others. It's a place of long-term familiarity, so irritations naturally arise. Home is a place that gets cluttered, that always needs straightening up and clearing out. It's a place that can fall apart from neglect.

Home provides challenge for life's biggest issues: performing vows, practicing faithfulness and daily discipline, revealing our true selves, stuffing the urge to run.

Home is a place where we experience all the seasons and moods—leaving no illusions as to the potential ferments and hidden faults—and declare it good, satisfying, worthy. It's a place where we dig our heels in and ask, "What can I do to make things better?"

Even when we know where home is, it's not always easy to stay there.

God Who Is Our Home

At some time in our lives we catch some glimpse of how little we count in the universe. We are minuscule, tiny nothings. The real world is gargantuan. This rude awakening both overwhelms us and can at the same time, reassure us. There has got to be more than us out there. There has got to be Someone bigger and smarter and more powerful. There has got to be Someone who has a big view, a clear picture, who knows what this is all about.

> But trailing clouds of glory do we come
> From God, who is our home. . . .[10]

The poet says we started with God, who is sunshine and light and glory, and ended in the womb, which is dark and empty. Then, we spend our lives trying to find Him again.

Theologians say we're born with a God-size vacuum in our hearts, that we must invite Him into that void made for Him, or we'll never be at peace, never truly find home. "O Lord, our hearts are restless until they rest in Thee," said St. Augustine.

We all have basic, driving needs: to be unconditionally loved—just as we are, regardless of performance; to have the hope that we can live forever, otherwise, we lose everything we treasure, and death never seems right; to find purpose and meaning to our existence—to know that what we do isn't useless, that we have lasting impact on the world.

Only God can entirely meet these needs.

Who is God? What is He like?

He is a Father wanting to reclaim His children, seeking to bring them back home.

He is a Father who is very powerful, but also deeply loving and personal. He is never boring. If we are bored, we're not close to our Father. He is infinitely creative "to think of new things to do together . . . for the next trillion ages of millenniums."[11]

He is a Father who makes rules that He expects to be obeyed. He is also merciful and forgiving.

He is a covenant maker and keeper. He is a very able provider. He is absolutely to be trusted.

He is a teacher, a Master. He is also a healer.

He is holy. He is awesome, even terrible (to us) in His holiness. Yet, He gave everything of Himself He had to give to help us find release from the torment of our enslaving sins. He wants to make us heirs of His riches.

He is good. He is just and fair. He is gracious.

He is a peacemaker. He helps mediate our messes. He is a shepherd to us lost sheep. He is tender "beyond explanation."[12]

He encourages us, embraces us, and opens our minds to the stores, the treasures of heaven and how to get the most benefit from life here on earth.

He is there when we need Him. He is there when we ignore Him. He is always near. He is never a runaway.

> God is first and foremost, above and beyond any-thing else, a father. . . . Jesus came to tell us that God is a father.[13]

Nothing weighs greater on God's heart than that we know Him as our Father.

We are His daughters, loved and enjoyed, just as we are. But He is not the Heavenly Permissive Parent. His love has no boundaries, but His warnings and cautions and carefully crafted commandments do. He never coddles our pride, our resistance to growing up, our sin.

He's not like us—He doesn't think the way we think, He doesn't respond the way we do to irritations and cri-ses. He's not limited and weak and reactive like we are. He is a perfect Father. He can be wholly trusted with whatever happens, with whatever we bring to Him.

He never abandons anyone on whom He has set
His love; nor does Christ, the good shepherd, ever lose
track of His sheep.[14]

Spiritual Runaways

Not everyone chooses to come home to the Father.

We can discipline our spirits to run from Him, to
reject His offer of love right up to our dying moment.
Chronic runaways lose their moral and spiritual com-
passes.

Rather than discover and accept who the Father
really is, we may prefer a manufactured composite of
what we want Him to be and what various people tell us.
Our feelings about God can drastically affect our ideas
of God.[15]

We may mistrust Him, hide from Him. We may tell
ourselves that He doesn't exist or that He doesn't really
know how to love, that He doesn't care, that He isn't
able to, or doesn't want to help us in our needs. This
brings the deepest loneliness of all.

Or we can try to meet Him just halfway. We want to
find Him, but resist His getting too close. We're not sure
what will be required of us. We're worried about exposure. We're fearful of the demands He'll make. We're
not sure of our reception. We're afraid to be completely
at home with Him. What is He like to live with? Will we
have any space, any life of our own? Can we ever
please Him? Is He tyrannical, possessive? Or is His "the
safest love there is?"[16]

Instead of running from Him, He wants to be our hiding place.

> You are my hiding place;
> > you will protect me from trouble
> > and surround me with songs of
> > > deliverance.
> > > > Psalm 32:7

Letting Him In

We find God in solitude. Just the two of us. No distractions. Getting to know Him through the Bible and direct contact. Sharing with Him every detail of our thinking and wanting and our appreciation. We find Him by diligent study and meditation of His communication to us, the record of His dealings with humankind through the ages, His personal message to us today: the Bible. We seek His friendship every day. As with any relationship, our major means of knowing Him better, and getting things done, is through communication.

Getting settled into a spiritual home is a daily exercise—seeking the face of our heavenly Father, asking that our needs be met, crying out to the Father on behalf of our hurting family members. Concentrated, regular contact helps us rid the distortions and barriers that keep us strangers, that make us reluctant to come home completely to Him.

We know we are not all the way home if:
- we can't relax in His presence
- we don't feel forgiven
- we have a hard time trusting our Father
- we're afraid to allow Him to help us with choices
- we're constantly full of doubts about His love, about His ability to provide, about His attention to our concerns, about His power to deliver

People down through the ages who dared to know God as home in the closest way possible have found Him to be good and gracious and a power base for doing great things for Him. "God held me by the hand," said Teresa of Avila in the 1500s. "I could hear His slightest whisper."[17]

The Bible says that we are really aliens and sojourners on this earth. Our real home is heaven. Security and confidence comes through knowing who we are, where we came from, and where we're going.

Elaine Nelson Thompson was adopted. She always feared seeking out who her natural mother and father were because, "If they rejected me once, they could reject me again. I couldn't bear that." Meanwhile, she endured abuse and a sense of not belonging in her adopted family. "I never felt I really had a home," she explains. But a national tragedy provided her an unusual insight.

"I was watching the news on TV and they were saying that large machinery would be used to remove the remaining debris and bodies of victims from the Oklahoma City nine-story federal building that had been bombed. The situation had become too dangerous for rescue workers to continue sifting by hand. My heart was so touched for the families whose loved ones were still in the rubble. Without a body, there was no closure. The tragedy was doubled for them.

"Later that evening I was reminded of my own heartache—not having any tangible evidence of my beginnings. But the Bible says I was created by God before the world began. By setting my mind on things 'above,' I can be encouraged and fulfilled regardless of my earthly situation.

"I can't find my roots. They can't find the evidence of their loved ones' ending. But to be absent from our bodies is to be present with the Lord. And I have the strongest roots anyone can have—in my heavenly Father. For the first time I began to understand the importance of my spiritual heritage, my spiritual home."

Coming home to God means seeing our world in a whole new vigorous way—enjoying the good and beautiful to the fullest extent, but also feeling the pangs of its corruptions and sorrows. We don't settle in and then go about our business. We settle in and learn how to go about His business.

God as our home is an irony. It means He comes to live with and in us. By His Spirit, He leaves His huge, golden mansion to reside in the cramped, dirty shack of our quarters. Then, He patiently cleans and expands this humble dwelling place, as we allow Him, when we're ready. At the same time, He's got a mansion in mind for us, next to His.

God is our ultimate home—our destination, as well as our present residence. God Himself is our home now and He is preparing a place where we will live with Him forever. One specially designed for us. One with our name. Our permanent address. Until we are found by Him, we're celestial fugitives.

But there's a hitch.

There's only one door to this home. Jesus the Son, our Brother, stands at that door. He sacrificed His perfect, sinless life to pay the debt for our sins.

He got punishment. We get peace. He got wounds. We get healed. He got separation from the Father. We get life, with Him, forever.

He could have run away. He wanted to. But He stayed and suffered it through for me and you. No one gets in without acknowledging, submitting to, making peace with Jesus Christ.

There are no homeless in heaven. No poor. No runaways.

All who live there want to be there. It's Home.

> Come home, come home,
> You who are weary, come home.

Discovery Questions

1. Write as many descriptive words as you can think of that explain your picture of what "home" is.

2. Can you imagine a situation in which you might become homeless?

3. Write a brief definition of each of the following. Which seems negative to you? Which are positive? Why?
   • transient
   • wanderer
   • pioneer
   • immigrant
   • emigrant
   • expatriate
   • drifter
   • homeless
   • runaway

4. In one paragraph, describe how God seems to you. Do you know Him as well as you'd like to?
If not, what can you do about it?

5. If possible, talk with a woman who ran away. Ask her why she went, what the outcome was—her regrets, her insights.

What repercussions continue to reverberate?
Where is her home now?

6. In what situations have you heard someone say something to this effect: "God is unreasonable," or "God expects the impossible," or "God does not provide adequate help"?
    What is your response?

7. Read Psalm 107:1–9. What does this say about finding a home?

8. Read Psalm 119:32 in as many translations as possible (NIV, KJV, AMPLIFIED, BERKELEY, NRSV). Which of these versions do you prefer, and why? What does this verse say to you?

9. Read Hebrews 11:13–16. When and where did these people find home?

10. Read Psalm 103, Hosea 2:19–20, 1 John 3:1–3.
    What does this say about God? How can we best respond to Him?

Notes

[1]Bharati Mukherjee, interview by Bill Moyers in *A World of Ideas*, vol. 2 (New York: Doubleday, 1990), 3.

[2]Ellen L. Bassuk, M.D., "Who Are the Homeless Families? Characteristics of Sheltered Mothers and Children," *Community Mental Health Journal* 26, no. 5 (October 1990): 425.

[3]Joan Abrams, "Laundromat Serves as Home for Mother, Son," *Lewiston* (Idaho) *Morning Tribune*, 25 November 1993, C1.

[4]Carol L. Bruning, "Practical Help for the Homeless," *World Vision*, April/May 1993, 7–8.

[5]Rene I. Jahiel, "The Situation of Homelessness," *The Homeless in Contemporary Society* (Newbury Park: Sage, 1978).

[6]Nancy Rubin, "America's New Homeless," *McCall's*, November 1988, 118-123.

[7]Ron Wilson, "The Rich Young Rulers," *World Vision*, October/November 1991, 19.

[8]Mukherjee, interview.

[9]Denis D. Haack, "Seeing Our Work the Way God Does," *Moody*, September 1989, 21.

[10]William Wordsworth, "Intimations of Immortality," Recollections of Early Childhood, in *Familiar Quotations*, by John Bartlett (Boston: Little, Brown, 1982), 426:14.

[11]John Piper, *The Pleasures of God* (Portland, Ore.: Multnomah Press, 1991), 195.

[12]Dan DeHaan, "What Motivates God?" *Moody*, February 1983, 70.

[13]Ibid., 71.

[14]J. I. Packer, *Knowing God* (Downers Grove, Ill.: InterVarsity Press, 1973), 79.

[15]David Seamands, "Healing Our Feelings about God," *Good News*, March/April 1986, 12.

[16]Henri J. M. Nouwen, "Running from What We Desire," *Partnership*, July/August 1986, 35.

[17]Deen, "Teresa of Avila—Beloved Woman of the Carmelites," *Great Women*, 105.

Note to the Reader

The publisher invites you to share your response to the message of this book by writing Discovery House Publishers, P. O. Box 3566, Grand Rapids, MI 49501, U.S.A. For information about other Discovery House books and music, contact us at the same address or call 1-800-653-8333.